"Pain is inevitable—but misery is optional. If you are miserable because of some addiction, some repetitive pattern of behavior that only brings you suffering, then opt for freedom. In *Healing the Scars of Addiction*, Dr. Jantz has provided the tools you need to heal, to overcome—to be free."

Timothy R. Jennings, MD, DFAPA, past president of the Tennessee and Southern Psychiatric Associations; author of *The Aging Brain*

"*Healing the Scars of Addiction* provides understanding, helpful steps, and realistic hope for those who are struggling with various forms of addiction and want to reclaim their lives from addiction and move forward into a healthier life. I highly recommend it!"

Siang-Yang Tan, PhD, professor of psychology, Fuller Theological Seminary; author of *Counseling and Psychotherapy: A Christian Perspective*

Books by Gregory L. Jantz, PhD,
with Ann McMurray

Healing the Scars of Emotional Abuse
Overcoming Anxiety, Worry, and Fear
Every Woman's Guide to Managing Your Anger
Healing the Scars of Childhood Abuse

Books by Gregory L. Jantz, PhD,
and Dr. Tim Clinton with Ann McMurray

Don't Call It Love

HEALING
THE
SCARS
OF
ADDICTION

Reclaiming Your Life *and*
Moving *into* a Healthy Future

GREGORY L. JANTZ PhD
with Ann McMurray

Revell
a division of Baker Publishing Group
Grand Rapids, Michigan

© 2018 by Gregory L. Jantz

Published by Revell
a division of Baker Publishing Group
PO Box 6287, Grand Rapids, MI 49516-6287
www.revellbooks.com

Printed in the United States of America

ISBN 978-0-8007-2773-4

Library of Congress Cataloging-in-Publication Control Number: 2018007049

Unless otherwise indicated, Scripture quotations are from the Holy Bible, New International Version®. NIV®. Copyright © 1973, 1978, 1984, 2011 by Biblica, Inc.™ Used by permission of Zondervan. All rights reserved worldwide. www.zondervan.com

Scripture quotations labeled KJV are from the King James Version of the Bible.

This publication is intended to provide helpful and informative material on the subjects addressed. Readers should consult their personal health professionals before adopting any of the suggestions in this book or drawing inferences from it. The author and publisher expressly disclaim responsibility for any adverse effects arising from the use or application of the information contained in this book.

In keeping with biblical principles of creation stewardship, Baker Publishing Group advocates the responsible use of our natural resources. As a member of the Green Press Initiative, our company uses recycled paper when possible. The text paper of this book is composed in part of post-consumer waste.

18 19 20 21 22 23 24   7 6 5 4 3 2 1

This book is dedicated to those struggling to overcome addiction: who try and fail, then try again; who stumble and fall and find a way to get back on their feet; who refuse to give up on their dreams of a better life; who cling to the hope they are worth that life—because they are.

Contents

The pathway of addiction is littered with questions. Should I stop? What will happen if I do stop? What will happen if I don't stop? Why should I stop? Why can't I stop? What have I done? When will this end? This book is written to give voice to these questions and provide hard-won answers gained from more than thirty years of working with courageous, addicted people. Those suffering from addiction need answers, but so do those who suffer alongside them.

A dictionary definition of *addiction* is simple: "a strong compulsion to have or do something harmful." Simple, or is it? Who defines what is harmful?

A strong compulsion to have or do something harmful covers a vast field of possibilities, given human invention and the capacity for denial. When even "good" things become harmful, the range of harmful things can multiply like mice. Besides the age-old options, people are addicted today in ways past generations couldn't have imagined.

Introduction

The Questions of Addiction

"This isn't the life I planned." The statement was made with dead-pan brevity. For a moment, I let his words hang in the air between us before I asked, "How is it different?"

In my work as a therapist, I operate within the borders of "different." People who have the life they've always dreamed of rarely end up in my office. Instead, I tend to work with those who come to the painful realization that all is not fine in their worlds. Some have tried to fix the different on their own but have failed. Others have no idea how to fix the different, beyond showing up for an appointment. Each knows that "here" isn't where they want to be, but they're not sure how to get somewhere else. I've found this is especially true when the here includes addiction.

I've worked with people who confidently thought they were immune to addiction. *That will never be me*, they thought—until it was. I've worked with some people who, as children, grew up around addiction and remember praying, *Please, God, don't let that be me*—until it was. I've worked with others who said yes to something, with no plans for it to change into something else—until it did.

Some have loved their addiction and viewed it like an engaging but unruly child. They wanted me to help them manage their addiction so they could keep it. Some have hated their addiction and wanted to find a way to destroy it without destroying themselves in the process. Others have wanted the addiction gone but felt lost, no longer knowing who they were and afraid that once the addiction was gone, they would cease to exist as well.

He started with a single statement about the life he'd planned. That statement prompted my question about how his life was different and went on to produce a cavalcade of additional, difficult questions. In my experience, the pathway of addiction is littered with questions. Should I stop? What will happen if I do stop? What will happen if I don't stop? Why should I stop? Why can't I stop? What have I done? When will this end?

This book is written to give voice to these questions and provide hard-won answers gained from more than thirty years of working with courageous, addicted people. When their lives turned out to be different from what they wanted, each found a way to ask difficult questions, to persevere and find needed answers. I can only assume the reason many of you picked up this book is to do the same. You are not yet where you want to be, and you're searching for a way to get there. My hope is, within these pages, you find markers of insight that help you along your path to healing from addiction.

If there is a consistent theme I've noticed among those who have healed from addiction, it is a deep desire to help others. Knowing firsthand motivates them to extend a hand up. The challenges and victories you'll read about in this book are compiled from their stories. While I've changed them enough to shield their identities, the core honesty, struggle, drive, and determination remain as encouragement and motivation for you. In a way, this is not my book or theirs or even yours, but ours together, as a broader community, seeking to heal the broken parts of lives around us, including our own.

The addiction community includes not only those who are addicted but also those who suffer alongside the addicted. I am speaking of mothers and brothers, sisters and fathers, cousins, aunts, uncles, and grandparents. I am speaking of the spouses, children, and fierce friends who love the addicted. These are the ones who watch the desolation of the addiction take hold, who try to change the person in ways both helpful and hurtful. These are the ones whose hearts break and pray, who turn away to save themselves but still look back.

If you love a person struggling with an addiction, I would say this book is for you. Yes, it is written to provide answers to the addicted, but by understanding their answers, you may find answers for yourself. Where addiction is concerned, there are more than enough questions and, hopefully, answers to go around and encompass us all. My hope is that by reading this book you will come to better understand the heart of the addicted person you love, because the scars of addiction that need healing are also your own.

He'd planned a different life. He hadn't anticipated becoming addicted to something that would slowly eat away at his health, his business, his family, and his relationships. He was ashamed and deeply fearful. During our time together, he alternately fought the desire to take blame on himself and to vigorously cast blame onto others. He struggled to come to terms with the addiction's consequences without giving in to his desire to minimize the damage. He battled to come to terms with those consequences without drowning in a sea of guilt. He might have quit; others have. Week after week, though, he kept coming, working through the pain.

When I think of recovery from addiction, the most descriptive word I've found is *healing*. The process of overcoming an addiction has always seemed to me to have similarities with overcoming a severe illness. Both take over your life and require intentional, difficult treatment. Both stretch the understanding and support of family and friends. Both have a brutal way of reordering priorities and laying your soul bare. Both have the potential for making you better today than you were yesterday in your human, if not always your physical, condition.

Addiction creates so many questions. What are the questions you have about addiction, your own or another's? Don't be afraid of the questions, no matter how painful they are to contemplate. Asking questions is how we come up with answers.

1

Am I an Addict?

"I'm not an addict," Madison told me confidently. "I can stop whenever I want."

"You just don't want to," I concluded.

"Yeah, I don't want to." At nineteen, Madison was living at home, not working or going to school, telling her parents she was still trying to "find" herself. The only reason she was in my office was because they had threatened to turn off the support spigot if she didn't. Addiction wasn't her problem, Madison asserted. The problem was her parents, who didn't trust her, expected her to follow stupid rules, and completely failed to understand why what she was doing was "no big deal."

"Why don't you want to stop?" I asked.

"Why should I? It's their problem, not mine."

"So, it is a problem. Is it their problem or yours that you're no longer in school?" Her parents had told me they had refused to cover any further tuition, as she routinely did not show up for classes or complete assignments. They were tired of what they called "throwing money away."

She shrugged and looked around my office. She avoided answering by saying, "I don't really know what I want to do."

"Oh, I think you know exactly what you want to do," I told her. For the first time, Madison stopped fidgeting and looked me straight in the eye.

Looking Addiction in the Eye

According to the American Society of Addiction Medicine (ASAM), addiction is characterized by:

- inability to consistently abstain (even when you know you should say no, you keep saying yes)
- impairment in behavioral control (the addiction takes over what you do and say so you become a different person than you were)
- craving (having is never enough; instead, you are left constantly wanting)
- diminished recognition of significant problems with one's behaviors and interpersonal relationships (you lose the ability to see how the addiction is ruining your life and relationships)
- dysfunctional emotional response (your emotions aren't in line with what is really happening and you're unable to figure out what your responses should be)[1]

The ASAM goes on to say that "like other chronic diseases, addiction often involves cycles of relapse and remission. Without treatment or engagement in recovery activities, addiction is progressive and can result in disability or premature death."[2] Addiction doesn't go away on its own. It doesn't get better; it gets worse. Pretending addiction doesn't exist ensures it does.

A dictionary definition of *addiction* is simple: "a strong compulsion to have or do something harmful." Simple, or is it? Who defines what is harmful? And to whom? Addiction throws up barriers to answering those questions about what is harmful.

The Barrier of Denial

Even asking the question "Am I am addict?" requires courage to overcome a huge first barrier of denial. Addiction is fueled by denial's stubborn power, the steadfast refusal to accept something is true. For weeks, Madison and I went round and round, trapped in a dance of denial. I kept trying to forge different pathways past denial and toward the truth; she kept boxing me out with sarcastic statements, meandering distractions, and smoldering hostility. Being an addict was not an identity Madison, at nineteen, wanted to claim.

Frankly, I couldn't blame her. Who would want to—at nineteen or any age? What she needed was help; what she wanted was to claim she could handle life on her own. She wanted to deny being an addict, but to heal Madison needed to admit she was.

Confronting an addict is a roll-of-the-dice proposition. Some flatly refuse to consider even the remote possibility. Others dissolve into a mass of recriminations, tears, and utter despair. Still others agree to entertain the notion while attempting to negotiate whether to continue.

There is a reason speakers at an Alcoholics Anonymous (AA) meeting begin with "Hello, my name is . . . and I'm an alcoholic." Admitting such a truth publicly catapults you over the barrier of denial. Once you've accepted that addiction is part of your life, you can use that truth to dictate what part the addiction will play in your life going forward.

Denial cannot be allowed to answer what is harmful.

The Barrier of Secrecy

Did you ever break something when you were a kid? A drinking glass, a lamp? If you were like me, the first thing you did was look around to see if anyone noticed. Next, you tried to hide the damage so it wouldn't be discovered. Addicts are very good at finding ways to hide, because addiction thrives in secrecy.

"You can't tell my parents," Madison told me. Willing, finally, to talk about her addiction, she still wanted to keep the truth hidden from her parents. "I don't want them to know how bad it is."

"You don't want them to know how bad you are," I amended, having learned Madison responded better to provocative statements. They tended to be met with corresponding bluntness on her part and an opportunity for some level of dialogue.

"They already think I'm a terrible person," she conceded.

"You're not terrible," I assured her, "but your addiction is. Your parents may not know all the details, but they do know that."

Secrecy provides cover, both to the addict and to the addiction, but secrecy's benefits are not the same for each. Secrecy allows the addiction to reveal what it truly is. Secrecy does not act to restrain the addiction; instead, it provides a platform of noninterference, a free-for-all. Conversely, while secrecy allows the addiction to reveal what it is, it allows the addict to hide who they are. An addiction feels no shame or remorse, but an addict can and will. Addiction thinks being restrained is harmful, so it operates in secret. Addicts think being exposed is harmful, so they act in secret.

Secrecy cannot be allowed to answer what is harmful.

The Barrier of Minimizing

Madison alternated between "things are so bad" she didn't want me to tell her parents and "things aren't so bad," so there was no need to tell her parents. We had to wrestle for a while before she could see that the goal in both of those opposites was not to tell her parents. Her life was broken and she wanted to keep the damage from them, through either outright secrecy or obscuring the truth by trying to minimize it.

When the thing you broke as a kid was invariably discovered, you could no longer keep the damage secret. Your only option was to minimize the damage, to make it seem less than it was. "We have plenty of glasses." "No one will notice the scratch if I turn the lamp this way." You used any reason you could come up with to try to avoid the consequences, which experience taught you were going to be negative.

Addiction doesn't travel far from those youthful minimizations. The consequences you're trying to minimize, however, can be much more severe than a broken glass or a scratched lamp. Unfortunately, as you get older, addiction can cause more destruction, but addicts can become more adept at minimizing the destruction.

Minimizing cannot be allowed to answer what is harmful.

The Barrier of Maximizing

Minimizing is an attempt to make the addiction seem less than it is. Maximizing is an attempt to make the addiction seem more than it is—more powerful, more inevitable. Maximizing is also called catastrophic thinking. From *Psychology Today*: "Catastrophic thinking can be defined as ruminating about irrational worst-case outcomes. Needless to say, it can increase anxiety and prevent people from taking action in a situation where action is required."[3]

In the defeatist thinking of maximizing, the addiction is so big that it's already won and attempting to change is a lost cause. The future becomes defined in failure, with success no longer up for grabs. "This is just the way I am" becomes the rationale for staying trapped within the addiction, which becomes the new normal.

After the power of the addiction has been maximized and deemed inevitable, I've seen something odd happen—the maximized is flipped into the minimized. What was so huge and terrible and inevitable becomes "just the way things are" and takes on a sense of normalcy. Normal has a way of seeming less terrible. When terrible becomes normal, the definition of terrible is downgraded. Maximization morphs into minimization.

Maximizing cannot be allowed to answer what is harmful.

The Barrier of Shame

Madison admitted her addiction much earlier than she admitted her shame. At first she attempted to wear her addiction like a badge of honor, with bravado completely consistent with her age. What took longer for her to truly admit was the depth of shame she felt about her addiction. Her shame, though, was eroding her sense of self and motivating her to remain numbed by the addiction. Until she was ready to explore those painful, shameful places, Madison remained tethered to her addiction.

Addiction exacts a toll on your sense of self. It causes you to do and say, to think and act in ways that humiliate you, embarrass you, harm you, and harm others. There can be great shame in admitting you are not in control and the addiction is. In a paradoxical way, admitting you have no control over your life is often the first step to taking control back. I don't think it's by chance that the first step to recovery in the Twelve Steps of Alcoholics Anonymous is an admission that you are powerless and your life has become unmanageable.[4]

Shame cannot be allowed to answer what is harmful.

Recognizing the Truth of Addiction

What is your truth? Are you able to recognize it? Has it become obscured by denial, shrouded in secrecy, deflated by minimization, or inflated by maximization? Are you worried you've wanted multiple times to stop but just can't seem to find the right time or reason? What is that thing or behavior? Can you name it, just to yourself?

If so, I encourage you to keep whatever that is in mind as you answer the following questions, based loosely on the "Am

I an Addict?" questions from Narcotics Anonymous (NA).[5] I've changed them so they aren't focused on a set of substances but, rather, on a specific set of feelings and behaviors that could apply to any number of potentially addictive things.

Be honest in your answers; search inside yourself to find the truth. A very wise man once claimed the truth could set a person free.[6] I wholeheartedly believe that, because I've seen truth unlock the door to freedom for others and have walked through that door myself.

I urge you to courageously and honestly answer the following questions about the thing(s) or behavior(s) you've identified as potentially addictive:

1. Do you try to keep what you do a secret from others?
2. Have you ever lied to others about what you do or how often you do it?
3. Would you rather spend time doing this than being with other people?
4. Do you avoid people who have expressed displeasure at what you do?
5. Has your personal, school, or work life suffered because of this?
6. Have you ever gotten into legal trouble because of it?
7. Have you ever gotten into financial trouble because of it?
8. Have you tried to reduce what you're doing as a compromise instead of stopping?
9. Have you ever questioned who you are as a person with this in your life?
10. If others are aware of what you do, are you defensive or hostile?
11. If others are aware of what you do, are you shameful or guilty?
12. Are you preoccupied thinking about this?

13. Do you feel justified using this as a reward for how difficult life is?

14. Are you afraid you'll always be this way and won't be able to change?

15. Does part of you want to change and part of you not want to change?

The presence of addiction, as NA says, isn't a numerical calculation based on check marks. It's a personal calculation based on the answers you gave to the questions above and how you felt as you answered them. If you're concerned about some thing or behavior and you're not sure about the presence of addiction, ask yourself just one more question: "Am I willing to stop, right now?"

Addiction will have an immediate reaction to that question—a strong and resolute no. This may be followed by all sorts of reasons and excuses, but the visceral reaction to the thought of being without whatever it is will be strongly negative. I encourage you to accept your reaction without trying to change its shape. The reaction exists; pretending it does not serves you no good.

Perhaps addiction has been part of your past, so you're familiar with this no reaction; you've felt it to the core of your being before. You may have kicked out some addictive thing or behavior in the past only to find a new addiction has taken up residence in a different part of your life. You're afraid if you kick this new one out, that other one will find a way back in. You may have come to accommodate this new addiction, determining it isn't as bad as the other. You may have a pattern of switching from addiction to addiction, trying to find which one won't create as many problems at any given time. But a "lesser" addiction is still an addiction. It's important to recognize that, because of the progressive nature of addiction, "lesser" won't stay that way.

My advice is to be attuned to your responses. Be aware of the reasons you give for why you don't really have an addiction or why what you're doing isn't really that bad or it's better than what you were doing before. Pay attention to what you're telling yourself, because that voice is the voice of addiction. When you can recognize that voice and its source, you're one step closer to recovering your own voice without addiction's overtones. More than anything, you must be more creative in envisioning success than an addiction is in projecting defeat.

Accepting Addiction

An addiction is a strong compulsion to do something harmful. Recovery from addiction starts with accepting both the strength of the compulsion and the amount of harm involved. Accepting an addiction is a tightrope walk in which one is carefully balanced between harsh reality and wishful optimism. The balance pole must be weighted heavily with truth. Truth helps a person walk the line of acceptance without falling into a world of despair, where recovery is too hard, or into a world of fantasy, where recovery appears impossibly easy. In my experience, recovery is neither too hard nor too easy. Instead, each person must find their balance by walking a middle path while holding tightly to the truth.

After months of work, two attempts at recovery, and three second chances, Madison finally began to integrate addiction into her reality. Her petulant stubbornness flipped to become her ally. She stopped fighting and found ways to embrace the truth. She came to accept that, even though she couldn't change her past, she didn't have to surrender her future to addiction.

"I'm an addict," she came to admit, with neither bravado nor blame.

"Yes, you are," I agreed. "Now, what are you going to do about it?"

So, what are you going to do about it?

2

Why This?

Derek was irritated. I wasn't a medical doctor, he bluntly reminded me, so it was none of my business what his physician prescribed. He was in my office to work on depression and intimated that if I didn't stick to my own business, he would leave. I agreed I wasn't a medical doctor but told Derek I knew addictions and, in my professional judgment, he was addicted to his pain medication. I believed the shame, hiding, and lies of that addiction were contributing to his depression, as was his sense of hopelessness about the addiction. He was realizing his priorities had shifted from those he loved to what he craved. Derek was a tough sell and kept coming back to how something given to him by his doctor couldn't be harmful. To convince him, I needed to show him how it could.

Treating the Whole Person

When I first started working in counseling, I intentionally became a licensed mental health therapist and an addiction professional. I saw people with mental health issues turn to substances or behaviors to self-medicate and then become addicted. I saw people with addictions who also had a host of ancillary mental health struggles. I saw mental health reasons for addictions and addictive reasons for mental health issues. I felt treating one without the other addressed only part of the picture and compromised the likelihood of successful recovery.

I also realized that addictive behaviors and mental health issues took a significant toll on the body. So, I specifically partnered with medical and nutritional health-care providers. As a Christian, I recognized the spiritual devastation that could occur with these complex conditions and included a faith component, when desired, in treatment. Combining mental health, chemical dependency, medical, nutritional, and faith-based professionals brought together what I came to call a "whole-person" approach to recovery. Over the past thirty years, I've been pleased to witness increasing numbers of people come to the same conclusion and recognize the benefit of this whole-person approach to healing and recovery.

I've also seen a change in how people view what constitutes addiction. Substances such as alcohol and illicit drugs have commonly been associated with addiction, but right before I founded The Center, singer Karen Carpenter died from anorexia. I remember the collective shock that behaviors concerning food—or lack thereof—could be addictive. Karen Carpenter's death from an eating disorder caused people to consider that other things could harbor the potential for addiction beyond a pill or a bottle.

Once Pandora's box of addiction was cracked open, a plethora of possibilities poured forth. Since then, behavioral or process addictions have solidly been recognized alongside substance addictions. Gone is the thinking that only something a person consumes can be addictive. "Behavioral science experts believe that all entities capable of stimulating a person can be addictive; and whenever a habit changes into an obligation, it can be considered as an addiction."[1]

Addictive Substances

A dictionary definition of *addiction* is "a strong compulsion to have or do something harmful." To me, the "have" points to substances and the "do" points to behaviors. Together, they cover a vast array of possibilities, with some researchers pointing to "all entities" as potentials for addiction. I agree with the all entities group. I've seen how the human capacity for invention, coupled with the human capacity for denial, can turn even good things into harmful ones. The range of potentially harmful things, then, multiplies like mice. I've watched people today be addicted in ways past generations couldn't have imagined, in ways I couldn't have imagined when I got into this field more than thirty years ago.

Listing all entities capable of stimulating a person would take more space than this book has. However, what I can share are the substances and behaviors I've seen at The Center that have ensnared people in addiction. Some may surprise you. I offer these as examples of what is possible—from substances and behaviors that are inherently "bad" to those that are, on the surface, "good." So often the danger isn't in the thing itself but in how and why that thing is used.

Alcohol

Since the time of the Bible, alcohol has been known for its medicinal purposes, with the apostle Paul even instructing Timothy to "use a little wine for thy stomach's sake."[2] However, the Bible also says, "Do not get drunk on wine, which leads to debauchery."[3] So, which is it—good or bad? Clearly, alcohol is a neutral substance; the difficulty comes in how you use it—in a strictly limited medicinal capacity, to get totally sloshed, or somewhere in between. The difficulty, as we'll talk about later, comes also from how your body reacts to alcohol. But if alcohol can be both good and bad, how do you know if you've crossed a line toward addiction? One simple way is to take the long-standing CAGE Questionnaire[4] by asking yourself the following four questions:

1. Have you ever felt you needed to Cut down on your drinking?
2. Have people Annoyed you by criticizing your drinking?
3. Have you ever felt Guilty about drinking?
4. Have you ever felt you needed a drink first thing in the morning (Eye-opener) to steady your nerves or to get rid of a hangover?

According to the National Institute on Alcohol Abuse and Alcoholism, answering yes to two of those questions is considered "clinically significant."[5] In my experience, answering yes to even one of those questions has significance and can indicate how close a person is to the line between harmless and harmful.

Narcotics

The term *narcotics* covers a broad spectrum of substances that affect mood or behavior. They include both naturally occurring opioids and opiates, such as opium, morphine, and heroin, as well as those synthetically produced, such as Oxycontin and its generic, oxycodone, hydrocodone, Demerol, Percodan, or any number of branded or generic pharmaceuticals. These narcotics can be used to produce a euphoric effect, but they are often used to relieve pain. When a narcotic is used to get high, this can be viewed as a bad use. But when a narcotic is used to relieve pain, this can be viewed as a good use.

The balance between good and bad in relation to these substances is razor thin.

> The abuse of and addiction to opioids such as heroin, morphine, and prescription pain relievers is a serious global problem that affects the health, social, and economic welfare of all societies. It is estimated that between 26.4 million and 36 million people

abuse opioids worldwide, with an estimated 2.1 million people in the United States suffering from substance use disorders related to prescription opioid pain relievers in 2012 and an estimated 467,000 addicted to heroin. The consequences of this abuse have been devastating and are on the rise. For example, the number of unintentional overdose deaths from prescription pain relievers has soared in the United States, more than quadrupling since 1999. There is also growing evidence to suggest a relationship between increased non-medical use of opioid analgesics and heroin abuse in the United States.[6]

Are you like Derek, who dismissed his addiction to his pain medication because it was prescribed by a physician? Have you found yourself going to different doctors, clinics, or emergency rooms and being untruthful to obtain additional pain medication?

Prescription and Over-the-Counter (OTC) Medications

Painkillers are not the only good medication that can turn, decidedly, bad. According to the National Institute on Drug Abuse (NIDA), "Some medications have psychoactive (mind-altering) properties and, because of that, are sometimes abused—that is, taken for reasons or in ways or amounts not intended by a doctor, or taken by someone other than the person for whom they are prescribed. In fact, prescription and over-the-counter (OTC) drugs are, after marijuana (and alcohol), the most commonly abused substances by Americans 14 and older."[7] NIDA includes opioids under commonly abused drugs but also lists categories such as central nervous system depressants (like Valium or Xanax); stimulants (dextroamphetamines and amphetamines, along with methylphenidates like Ritalin or Concerta); and sedatives (barbiturates) and tranquilizers.[8]

Having a prescription written by a doctor does not protect someone from abusing such medication, especially when they don't follow the physician's medication orders. A Stanford University study showed that "over 60 percent of Americans don't follow doctors' orders in taking prescription meds."[9] How could researchers know this? They used seventy-six thousand urine samples taken from doctors' offices and cross-referenced whether each sample reflected the appropriate amount of medication. Sixty-three percent of people "strayed from their doctor's orders."[10] About a quarter of those studied did not take their prescribed medications at all, because they didn't want to, couldn't afford them, or unfortunately, were selling them to others. Overall, almost 40 percent were taking types and amounts not specifically prescribed for them by their physician.

Good drugs—and not just prescribed medications—can become harmful for a variety of reasons. I've also seen misuse occur in OTC medication. For example, I've run across people, without colds, who buy OTC cold medicine to use as a sedative or to get high through either dextromethorphan or simply the alcohol content. I've seen people who are addicted to diet pills or laxatives. Even motion sickness medication, such as Dramamine or Benadryl, can be used to produce a high. In fact, some stores have begun to pull these products from their general shelves and place them within the control of store personnel or back behind the pharmacy counter.

What about you? Are you taking prescription or OTC medication incorrectly? If so, for what purpose? And have you told your prescribing physician, or are you keeping your use a secret?

Tobacco

Information about smoking's and nicotine's harmful effects has been known for half a century. I remember the uproar when cigarette commercials were banned on television and radio when I was in middle school.[11] Yet according to the Centers for Disease Control and Prevention (CDC), in 2015, 15 percent of US adults smoked and "cigarette smoking is the leading cause of preventable disease and death in the United States, accounting for more than 480,000 deaths every year, or 1 of every 5 deaths."[12]

Why do people, knowing this information for years, still smoke? The addictive ingredient in tobacco is nicotine. "Nicotine, found in all tobacco products, is a highly addictive drug that acts in the brain and throughout the body. Dip and chew contain more nicotine than cigarettes. Holding an average-sized dip in your mouth for 30 minutes can give you as much nicotine as smoking three cigarettes."[13]

People use tobacco because tobacco is addictive. I've worked with people who were addicted to a variety of substances and have been told, more than once, that it was harder to quit cigarettes than hard drugs such as heroin. Just because you can buy one at a mini-mart and not the other doesn't mean much when it comes to addiction.

Caffeine

Generally, when people talk about caffeine, they're talking about caffeinated drinks, such as coffee, tea, and soda. But caffeine is also found in chocolate and foods that use chocolate or coffee as flavorings, including ice cream and yogurt.[14] People aren't always aware of the amount of caffeine in some of these products. Then there are products that openly use caffeine as a stimulant, such as "energy" drinks and diet pills. Caffeine is used to speed up metabolism, which burns more calories and makes a person feel more energized.

So, with all of that, is caffeine good or bad? According to the Mayo Clinic, caffeine has gotten a bad rap in years past. "Coffee has been around for a long time and blamed for many ills—from stunting your growth to causing heart disease—but newer research shows it may actually have health benefits. . . . In fact, some studies have found an association between coffee consumption and decreased mortality and possibly cardiovascular mortality, although this may not be true in younger people who drink large amounts of coffee."[15]

It seems the answer to whether caffeine is good or bad is "it depends." The Mayo Clinic goes on to say, "Studies have shown that coffee may have health benefits, including protecting against Parkinson's disease, type 2 diabetes and liver disease, including liver cancer. Coffee also appears to improve cognitive function and decrease the risk of depression." On the downside, they cite risks such as mild increases in cholesterol from drinking large amounts of unfiltered (boiled or espresso) coffee. There is also, apparently, a "fairly common" genetic condition that can cause people with it to break down caffeine in the body more slowly, increasing their risk of heart disease if they have more than two cups of coffee a day.[16]

Is caffeine addictive? Again, I think the answer is "it depends." One individual we worked with drank ten to twelve pots of coffee per day—pots, not cups. I've known people who didn't drink any water; their sole source of liquids was coffee, tea, or soda. Upon waking in the morning, they headed straight for a caffeinated drink and relied on that boost throughout the day. While the physical effects of caffeine are slight, compared to other substances on this list, I still believe people can become dependent on caffeine for not only physical effects but also psychological comfort and routine.

A man I know in his fifties recently had an episode of atrial fibrillation. This man keeps to a healthy weight and exercises regularly. At the emergency room, he was cautioned by the doctor to stop consuming caffeine as a preventative measure. Here was a man, already disciplined in eating and exercise, who confessed he wasn't sure he could give up his coffee, even to avoid another trip to the emergency room.

Too much of any good thing can be harmful. The trick with caffeine, I believe, is to know when you reach that too much stage. For him, too much became any at all. For others, too much may be two cups a day if they have that genetic factor. For still others, too much may be drinking caffeinated drinks all day long. I believe addiction sets in when a person refuses to acknowledge that too much point. Have you been able to acknowledge and live within yours?

Food

Food is a powerful mood-altering substance. I say that as a person who loves to eat as well as a professional who deals with all types of eating disorders. I say that as a person who works with health-care professionals and dietitians schooled in the intricate connections between the food we eat and the way we feel. Food, at its physical level, is nutrition, fuel for life. But human beings aren't just bodies; we're also hearts and minds, intellect and emotions. Food intersects with all aspects of our whole person.

As a certified eating disorder specialist,[17] I find it possible to forget that a relatively small number of people are diagnosed with eating disorders. The statistics from the National Association of Anorexia Nervosa and Associated Disorders (ANAD) puts the numbers at just under 1 percent of women over their lifetimes for anorexia, 1.5 percent of women over their lifetimes for bulimia, and 2.8 percent of all adults for binge eating disorder over their lifetimes.[18] I must juxtapose those numbers with what I see in my practice, which are the high numbers of people who struggle with weight issues in general. According to the National Institutes of Health, "More than two-thirds (68.8 percent) of adults are considered overweight or obese. More than one-third (35.7 percent) of adults are considered to be obese. More than 1 in 20 (6.3 percent) have extreme obesity. Almost 3 in 4 men (74 percent) are considered to be overweight or obese."[19]

A small minority of people have an eating disorder, but I've found that too many people struggle with their weight. They struggle with using food for all sorts of reasons that have nothing to do with nutrition. I have found people (including myself at times) who eat to relieve stress and for comfort, who use physical fullness to compensate for emotional voids, who use food as a reward and sometimes as the one thing they feel they have control over. Food is perhaps the most readily available and socially acceptable mood-altering substance there is.

How do you use food? Do you view what you eat—or what you don't—from a nutritional point of view? Are you at war with your body? Do you deprive your body of the nutrients it needs through consuming either too much of the wrong things or too little of the right things? Do you even know, or care to know, the difference?

Supplements

This is a category that might be surprising to some. I am a proponent of appropriate nutritional supplementation. At The Center, we have medical and naturopathic physicians who routinely prescribe nutritional supplements to help with a variety of physical and psychological conditions. I've added supplements to the list because I've also seen people become addicted to taking them. One woman we worked with arrived on our doorstep with a shopping bag full of nutritional supplements. If one was good, she felt, two were better, and four surely would bring about the miraculous results she craved. She arrived with dozens of bottles and jars, canisters and containers, without any real understanding of how one interacted with another. She wasn't so much addicted to the supplements themselves as she was to the idea of what supplements might do.

This reliance on an addition from the outside to solve a deficit on the inside is at the core of addiction. Some people use alcohol, some use drugs, others use food, and this woman used supplements. If she could only take enough, the problems in her life would be solved and she could be happy—or, at least, not so sad and in pain. Asking anything to have that kind of power over your life is an invitation to addiction.

Addictive Behaviors

As a therapist and an addiction professional, I should be immune to addictions—or so you would think. And for the most part, my education and training did steer me clear of a great many pitfalls. That is, until I was blindsided by a situation straight out of my education and training. Early in my career, I became a workaholic. I was addicted to working, to striving, to trying to do more and be more and accomplish more. I went headlong from studies to internships to work, with no stopping in between; I took no days "off" from accomplishing my goals.

For some of you, this may seem like a strange addiction. What could be bad about always trying to do your best? I, however, thought the best was the only way I could be. I became the center of my world. My work. My accomplishments. My vision. The people I interacted with were those I was counseling. I had no children. I also brought my wife into that world right along with me. Anything—even people—outside my job began to be a distraction. My career was a heady, roller-coaster ride of goals, dreams, and accomplishments. With such a narrow vision, I lost perspective. I experienced profound burnout and had to find my way back to balance and spiritual purpose.[20] Going through that time in my life led me to a renewed passion for my work and a personal understanding of the power of an addictive behavior.

The thing that took over my life was work and obtaining the "prize" at the end of each day. In behavioral or process addictions, I've found there is always a prize. It is a sense of satisfaction gained, relief of disaster averted, or a combination of both. As you look over the following examples of behavioral addictions I've witnessed, please consider your own prize. When you do whatever it is that has an addictive hold on you, what do you hope to gain? What do you hope to avoid? The promise of gain is certainly part of behavioral or process addictions, but so is fear of loss. As you read over this list, keep your own gain and loss in mind.

Gambling

In my experience, a gambling addiction is all about payoff, but the payoff can be more than just money. For some people, gambling's "big win" may be about vindication and life finally going their way. In the single stroke of a big win, the planets align and you're rewarded beyond your expectations. Afterwards, you continue to gamble because you're looking for that lightning to strike again, to once again have fate acknowledge you are special and favored.

For others, gambling's payoff may be more about the thrill of risk. Winning or losing isn't the issue; playing the "game of chance" is. The thrill of uncertainty, of winning or losing, is the issue. You continue to gamble because it's the one unpredictable thing in your life, with the payoff being either the thrill of victory or the agony of defeat. Gambling, whether you win or lose, and the risk involved make you feel alive.

Gamblers engage in gambling because the activity itself is pleasurable. The euphoric "hit" this activity produces doesn't come from an outside substance. It comes from the inside, from your own brain chemicals—primarily dopamine. Gambling feels good because your brain is wired to produce dopamine during pleasurable activities. Researchers continue to study the role of dopamine, the brain's "reward" chemical, in responses to gambling and pathological gambling as well as in other behavioral addictions.[21]

If you're a gambler, what do you like about gambling? When do you get that hit of pleasure? Is it during a big win, or is it ongoing, as you experience the thrill of the unexpected? Do you gamble to feel more alive, or do you gamble to flee from real life?

Sex

Sex can make you feel good. For people who are addicted to sex and sexual activities, that good feeling doesn't last long enough. The satisfaction is too fleeting and the feeling must be addressed again—immediately. Some have described their sexual addictions as insatiable. Engaging in sexual activities seemed to make them crave more. Sex and the pursuit of sex is a constant loop in their minds. To engage in the sexual activity of their choice, they will reorder their priorities until every other part of their lives becomes subordinate to sexual gratification.

People I've counseled with sex addictions are often bewildered that their addiction has taken such control over their lives. They are humiliated by what they've done to satisfy sexual cravings, deeply shameful they are so enslaved to these activities. They are devastated at the damage their addiction has caused others, even when those people are unaware. While The Center sees more males with sexual addiction issues, we also work with females seeking recovery. When sexual satisfaction becomes linked to unhealthy motivations and behaviors, the strength of the addiction increases, especially within the secrecy that can shroud such compulsions.

Are you concerned you're addicted to experiencing sexual gratification? Do you think about sex or sexual activities during the day, to the disruption of other endeavors? Do you feel a sense of shame about your need to be sexually satisfied? Do you feel you are violating moral or religious principles to obtain sexual satisfaction?

Relationships

Sexual addiction is different from relationship addiction and needs to be considered separately. Sexual addiction is focused on sexual satisfaction. Relationship addiction is focused on a relationship, which may or may not contain a sexual component. People can become addicted to a parental relationship, a sibling relationship, a child relationship, or a friendship.

Relationship addiction is a condition in which you must be either in or pursuing a relationship to feel good about yourself or to avoid feeling bad about yourself. You derive your sense of identity and purpose through a relationship. Without a relationship, you become nothing. Relationships are your way of coping with life. You crave validation and a sense of wholeness—feelings you find impossible to experience on your own—through the relationship.

Do you gain an unhealthy amount of validation through being in relationship with another person? Are you fearful of being alone? Do you need others to make you feel valuable or worthwhile?

Recently, I wrote a book with Dr. Tim Clinton, president of the American Association of Christian Counselors, on relationship addiction titled *Don't Call It Love: Breaking the Cycle of Relationship Dependency*. Dependence on or addiction to relationships is a complex equation consisting of many factors. If you believe you are unduly reliant on a single relationship or on relationships in general, I urge you to consider reading that book as well.

Work

I mentioned before about the time in my career when I gained too much of my identity and self-worth from my work. I was no longer a human being; I was a "human doing." For some, the risks and rewards of job and career can be like those of a gambling addiction; either you're chasing the big win of that next deal or promotion, or you're energized by the heady unpredictability of success or failure. Still others work out of a dogged determination to do anything to avoid an inevitable lurking disaster.

Work becomes less a measure of income and more a measure of worth. Work becomes who you are instead of what you do. Other considerations get pushed out of the way in pursuit of this identity. If the thought of not working makes you feel diminished, less of a person, less valuable, and more vulnerable, you need to consider the possibility that you have an addiction. If you consistently find yourself placing your job above all other priorities in your life—such as family, friends, faith, or rest—your job may be taking more out of you than you are getting out of your job.

Anger and Negativity

I put these two behaviors together because I believe the first fuels the second. Do you know someone who seems angry all the time? Who responds to people and circumstances with hostility, sarcasm, or criticism? Are you familiar with someone who is quick to yell and bite back? Who seems to erupt over mere inconveniences? Are you acquainted with someone who always has a "but" for anything positive or takes pride in predicting disaster when everyone else is sure of success? Do you know someone who boasts about new offenses and takes them on almost enthusiastically? I believe these responses of anger and negativity come from a place of deep pain. The person's emotional "skin" is so raw and hurting, the slightest touch produces an instinctive, reactive response.

Some people, fearful of provoking such a reaction, learn to "walk softly" around an angry, negative person. If others respond in anger, the original anger becomes validated and can escalate. Conversely, some people can become so accustomed to receiving angry and negative overreactions that they cease to react at all. In this catch-22, when others respond, more anger becomes necessary. And when others fail to respond, more anger becomes necessary. This creates a spiral of anger and negativity, which is difficult to exit.

Do you consider yourself an angry person? Are other people afraid to express opinions around you? Do you often find yourself raising your voice or pointing your finger around other people or around certain people? Is it more difficult for you to say something positive than it is to say something negative? When you make positive statements about others, do you feel you're being insincere or inauthentic? Are you able to find more things wrong with a person or a situation than are right?

Passive-Aggressive Behavior

Passive-aggressive behavior is no less aggressive, though passivity is its first face. Passive-aggressive behavior, like anger and negativity, can become a conditioned response to life. Passive-aggressive people seek to avoid direct conflict with others. Instead, they find alternate ways to communicate their hostility. They might agree to a task but put off doing it. They might "forget" to fulfill an obligation. They might neglect giving an important piece of information.

They will disavow being angry. If confronted by something negative they've done or said, they might push it off as only joking, not intentional, or the result of a misunderstanding. When obligated to say something positive, they will find a way to sneak in a negative. Instead of openly confronting another person, they will talk negatively about that person to others.

Passive-aggressive behavior can be addictive because it's like playing adult hide-and-seek. The goal is to avoid having others "find" your truly negative feelings. Your goal is to find creative, satisfying ways to hide your anger, rage, resentment, disappointment, frustration, or irritation while still being clever enough to express them. As a bonus, the cleverer you are, the more deniability you build into your negativity. You consistently present as the moderate, reasonable person, with the other person perennially at fault for overreacting or misunderstanding. Passive-aggressive behavior becomes a satisfying, engaging, and perpetual game of behind-the-back "gotcha."

Risk

I've already mentioned risk in gambling, but risk-seekers can become addicted to much more than gambling. Risk-seeking becomes addictive when the risk behaviors cross the line into danger or obsession. Helping a person understand a risk-seeking addiction can be difficult because people have such different ways of evaluating risk.

One person I counseled was a mountain climber. We have some beautiful mountains in the Pacific Northwest, and mountain climbing in and of itself isn't pathological. However, mountain climbing, for him, became an addiction and was interfering with his life. The key to him understanding how this hobby had become an obsession was in tracing the progression. He first started climbing mountains with a group of college friends. They'd go out a couple of times a year whenever the weather was right. They had as much fun in the preparation, the drive up, the camaraderie on the slopes, and the ride home as they did summiting the peak of whatever mountain they were climbing.

Over the course of the next ten or so years, things changed. For this man I counseled, the peaks became too routine, the routes too well traveled. The laughing and joking of the others started to be irritating, distracting him from the true goal of pushing himself, besting himself, and testing himself against the odds. On the trips, he became intense, moody, rigid.

His buddies started to find reasons to avoid these excursions until he was accomplishing the climbs alone—and glad to be doing so. He went from making these solitary climbs a couple of times a year to as many weekends as he could manage. If the weather was lousy, he'd rage. When he fell on a climb and broke an ankle, he fumed and felt terrible about himself. The day came when he realized the only time he truly felt alive was when he was risking his life on a mountain. He knew he'd crossed a line but wasn't sure where or why.

Risk has been called an adrenaline rush. Here is how the website LiveStrong.com defines what happens in an adrenaline rush:

> When you perceive something as threatening or exciting, the hypothalamus in the brain signals to the adrenal glands that it's time to produce adrenaline and other stress hormones. The adrenal glands produce adrenaline by transforming the amino acid tyrosine into dopamine. Oxygenation of dopamine yields noradrenaline, which is then converted into adrenaline. Adrenaline binds to receptors on the heart, arteries, pancreas, liver, muscles and fatty tissue. By binding to receptors on the heart and arteries, adrenaline increases heart rate and respiration, and by binding to receptors on the pancreas, liver, muscle and fatty tissue, it inhibits the production of insulin and stimulates the synthesis of sugar and fat, which the body can use as a fuel in fight-or-flight situations.[22]

Risk is a compelling emotional and physical experience capable of inducing addictive responses.

Exercise

Stretching yourself to your physical limit doesn't require a mountain. Sometimes all it requires is a stretch of road and a good pair of shoes or early morning hours and a neighborhood gym. Exercise can become both physically and psychologically addicting. The physical addiction comes because the body is designed to tolerate intense physical exertion by producing natural opiates called endorphins.

Endorphin is a merging of two words—*endogenous*, meaning growing from within, and *morphine*.[23] The body's production of endorphins is responsible for what is known as "the runner's high," when a runner pushes past the point of endurance (called "hitting the wall") and reaches the euphoric other side. As a runner, I've experienced this sensation, and to be honest, it feels good.

Exercise can be psychologically addictive when exercising itself or the physical results are woven too tightly into a person's sense of identity, value, and worth. Sometimes exercise takes on a sacrificial role. If you eat "too much," you must sacrifice your body through exercise to atone. Exercise, when viewed as a sort of self-purifier, as a sacrifice for some sort of wrong or to achieve some sort of righteousness, can be addictive.

The addictive aspects of exercise have always played a role in the purging behaviors associated with eating disorders. After eating the "wrong" things or, in the case of anorexia, eating at all, those with an eating disorder search for a way to purge the body. Some people do this by inducing vomiting; others do it by restricting caloric intake thereafter; and others purge through exercise.

Physical movement and exercise are beneficial to the human body. Exercise becomes bad when done to the point of exhaustion, pain, or injury, or when a person feels excessive guilt if they are unable to exercise. Exercise can become a compulsion, a way for a person to deal with other things in life that are out of their control.

Shopping

Some people find their risks on the side of a mountain. Others seek out wins and losses in the aisles or on the websites of their favorite retailers. Scoring that perfect item can produce the same chemical hit as winning a jackpot. I've found that for those with a shopping addiction, the goal is to receive a sense of reward and pleasure, whether purchasing for themselves or for someone else.

However, as with all addictions, the reward and pleasure are fleeting; they don't last and must be endlessly replicated.

A person addicted to shopping has so many clothes, for example, that they can't possibly wear them all, let alone fit them into a single dresser or closet. They give away new clothes with the tags still on to make room for more. They can't remember what they have and may purchase the same thing multiple times. They may buy for children, grandchildren, and friends, foisting wanted—or unwanted—items onto others. They spend thousands of dollars without any real satisfaction.

One woman I know had hundreds of pairs of shoes. Another refused to wear the same outfit twice and shopped to make sure she never did. Addicted shoppers don't buy only clothes or shoes, of course. They buy whatever they perceive makes them feel good and, more importantly, safe. They shop not because they need something but because they need to *feel* something.

Technology Addictions

I've placed the following in their own category because I believe technology has the power to literally rewire our brains. Over the past few decades, I've watched society—and my own life and work—get turned upside down by the introduction of various forms of technology. When I said earlier that there are now ways to become addicted that previous generations couldn't have dreamed of, part of what I was referring to was the advent of and potential for addictive technology.

Television

Even with the internet and diminished interest in traditional broadcast media, it's still possible to be addicted to television for the same reasons television has always been compelling. Television is an engaging way to become unengaged. My generation called it "vegging," as in "vegging out" in front of the television—sitting virtually motionless for hours. I fight this sometimes. If my family is gone and the house is quiet, I'll reach for the remote, even when I don't have anything I particularly want to watch. Quiet can sometimes seem intimidating. Noise and distraction are familiar, and few things provide noise and distraction like television, which is a passive form of entertainment. The only thing I need to do with the television is turn it on and maybe turn the channel. If I don't want to think about something, if I want to numb out for some reason, the television is right there.

We have become a sedentary culture in our work, but we've also become quite sedentary in our leisure. According to a recent study, Americans watch an average of almost five hours of television per day.[24] I imagine that over the course of the next twenty years, that number will change as older generations leave the stage and younger techy generations alter the percentages. While the hours may switch from a television screen to screens in general, I don't think this large amount of screen time bodes well for our sedentary natures or our propensity to want to zone out from life.

Do you turn on the television out of habit, without any specific desire to watch? When you think about doing something unpleasant or uncomfortable, will you put that off by turning on the television? How many hours per day do you spend watching television? How much of that is spent sitting? How often are you frustrated when you realize you could have been doing something else instead of watching television?

Internet

If you want to talk about distraction, it's impossible to ignore the internet. The internet, for me, is a digital black hole, capable of sucking up vast amounts of my time. I can sit down (yes, sit) to quickly research an issue or look for a piece of information, only to come up for air hours later. If I want to be distracted from an unpleasant thought or emotion, I've got millions of places I can go to push those right out of my head and heart. The internet has virtually no limits. I can get as lost inside the internet as I choose.

For those who are tired or disappointed with life, the internet is a place to hide away from their own lives and a bedroom window into the private lives of others. Unlike when using social media, when you explore the internet, you can be as disconnected from other people as you want, without the need for posting or replies. You can look but don't have to touch, scrolling through pages and pages of anonymous (except to your internet service provider), self-directed data.

Social Media

Someone I know gave up Facebook when she realized she was spending close to forty hours per week living her life online. Forty hours per week seems like a lot of time but works out to be just fewer than six hours per day. Six hours per day doesn't seem like that much if you consider that people spend five hours per day watching television.

According to the Pew Research Center, 68 percent of all US adults use Facebook, 28 percent use Instagram, 26 percent use Pinterest, 25 percent use LinkedIn, and 21 percent use Twitter. Of the Facebook users, more than three-fourths (76 percent) went on-line daily, up 6 percent from just the previous year. Using multiple platforms is increasingly popular, with 29 percent of Facebook users also using Twitter, 39 percent also using Instagram, 36 percent also using Pinterest, and 33 percent also using LinkedIn. For those not on Facebook, 65 percent on Twitter also use Instagram and 49 percent of those on Instagram also use Twitter, 54 percent also use Pinterest, and 57 percent of Pinterest users also use Instagram.[25]

And that's just what's available at this moment in time. Tomorrow's must-have, must-do thing hasn't been invented yet—but it will be.

Social media appears to be a compilation of billions of users all coming together to connect. The energy, information, and connections involved with that many people are compelling and, for some, addictive. But the companies that provide social media have ways to additionally prime the addiction pump through notifications and algorithms. In an article on Computerworld titled "Social Media Addiction Is a Bigger Problem than You Think," Mike Elgan writes, "Notification numbers appear on the app icon to draw you in, then on the top or bottom menu to draw you in further. . . . You've got to click or tap. It's compulsive. And over time, it becomes addictive."[26] Regarding the effect of algorithms, he says, "The biggest tool in the social media addiction toolbox is algorithmic filtering. Sites like Facebook, Google+ and, soon, Twitter, tweak their algorithms, then monitor the response of users to see if those tweaks kept them on the site longer or increased their engagement. We're all lab rats in a giant, global experiment."[27]

Just as cigarette companies found ways to make their products more addictive, social media companies do the same. The only difference is cigarette companies used nicotine, an outside substance, to increase addiction while social media companies use our internal neurochemicals to reinforce us to consume their products. We have become Pavlov's dogs, salivating when we see that notification and then clicking.

Within a few years, social media has created within humans an almost insatiable desire to be online. There is now even a name for returning to social media after swearing to give it up. The term is *social media reversion*, and it is defined in a recent survey as "when a user intentionally ceases using a social media site but then later resumes use of the site."[28] The study found four "themes" that contributed to an increased likelihood of reversion: perceived addiction, boundary negotiation, mood, and other social media.

Perceived addiction included experiences such as feelings of withdrawal when not using and loss of self-control. Boundary negotiation emphasized those users who felt a need to use for "impression management"; in other words, they felt compelled to go online to make sure they could manage their digital identity. Mood was simply that people were more likely to go back to using social media if doing so made them feel better than when they didn't use it. And, finally, reversion was affected by whether people utilized other social media outlets to compensate for staying off one.[29]

Are you on Facebook, Instagram, Pinterest, or one of the other social media sites? How often do you go online to check your account? Are you there to post or to view? Do you find yourself going on for just a few minutes but then spending much more time than you anticipated? What are you not doing so you can spend time on social media? Have you told yourself you need to cut down on the time you spend on social media but find you're unable to do so? Are you worried you'll miss something important if you don't keep checking?

Video Games

"At an addiction treatment center in Amsterdam, the Netherlands, teenagers and young adults begin detox by admitting they are powerless over their addiction."[30] So starts an article on addiction on WebMD. When I think of Amsterdam, the addiction that immediately comes to mind is drugs, with images of glassy-eyed youths sprawled on the streets or huddled in doorways. The next sentence quickly dispels those images: "But these addicts aren't hooked on drugs or alcohol. They are going cold turkey to break their dependence on video games."[31] The article goes on to quote Dr. Kimberly Young, internet addiction specialist and clinical director of the Center for On-Line Addiction. "I've had so many parents call me over the last year or two, particularly about the role-playing games online. I see it getting worse as the opportunity to game grows—for example, cell phone gaming," Young says.[32] These games, just like social media, are specifically designed to draw people in and keep them there. A fascinating analysis on 425Business explains that "MMOs (massively multiplayer online role-playing games) rely on the three prongs of the self-determination theory of motivation: autonomy, competence, and relatedness. . . . Everything is in the numbers. It's what level you are, what equipment you've got, what stat bonuses you have, and so forth. And seeing friends pop up with their online status and invite you to a group—it's all very satisfying."[33] It's all very satisfying—until it's the only thing that's satisfying. When that happens, an addiction is born.

Pornography

It's hard to choose where to put pornography as an addiction. I chose to place it here, under technology, because of the shift in the availability and use of pornography due to technology. The internet combines an inexhaustible supply of pornographic material, the psychological and technical savvy of porn providers, the anonymity of digital consumption, and the accessibility of devices.

A couple of years ago, pornography rates made the news when a Barna Group study reported that "64 percent of Christian men and 15 percent of Christian women admitted to viewing pornography at least once a month, compared to 65 percent of men and 30 percent of women who identified as non-Christian and said they watched porn at the same rate."[34] Pornography, for some, is an activity, not an addiction. That's not how I see it from my vantage point as a professional counselor. At The Center, we treat people who come in because of an addiction to pornography, who have all the hallmarks of classic addiction—compulsion to engage, withdrawal when not engaged, tolerance, mood modification, and inability to cut down or stop even when faced with negative consequences.

Because of the shame experienced by some regarding this addiction, especially those raised within a religious structure, we sometimes don't learn the truth about the pornography addiction until well into treatment for other issues. Pornography, like sex addiction, can be shrouded in secrecy and tangled with an addiction to technology and the internet.

Cell Phones

How can you become addicted to something you need every day? Or is that another definition of addiction? I confess to being tethered to my cell phone, which is the nexus point for my ability to communicate (along with my Apple Watch). I struggle to keep that connection to my cell phone under control, and I am not alone.

According to a recent National Institutes of Health study reported in *Frontiers in Psychiatry*, "The problematic use of cell phones has been associated with personality variables, such as extraversion, neuroticism, self-esteem, impulsivity, self-identity, and self-image. Similarly, sleep disturbance, anxiety, stress, and, to a lesser extent, depression, which are also associated with Internet abuse, have been associated with problematic cell-phone use. In addition, present review reveals the coexistence relationship between problematic cell-phone use and substance use such as tobacco and alcohol."[35]

I don't really need research studies to convince me of the impact of cell phones. All I need to do is watch groups of people—on the street, in restaurants, at the library, waiting for a bus—use their cell phones. You can see the impact, even in a movie theater, where you're supposed to disconnect for a few hours. I see people everywhere focused peripherally on their surroundings but more intensely focused on their cell phones. When the first iPhone came out about a decade ago, videos surfaced of people walking off curbs and into posts, traffic, mall fountains, and all sorts of hazards because they were engrossed with their phones. (A similar phenomenon occurred in 2016 with the release of the popular game Pokémon Go.)

Anything that engrossing has the potential for addiction. I really like this analogy from Dr. David Greenfield, director of the Center for Internet and Technology Addiction: "Right before [people] go to bed, the last thing they do before they pass out is check their phone and the minute they open their eyes, they check their phone. Doesn't that sound like a smoker? This is what we used to hear with smokers is that the last thing they would do before they go to bed is they'd have their last cigarette."[36]

Do you routinely check your cell phone right before you go to bed? Do you sleep with your cell phone next to you? Do you check your cell phone first thing in the morning? If you left your cell phone at home, would you leave work to retrieve it? How long have you gone without checking your cell phone? Do you feel somehow incomplete without your cell phone? Do you routinely give your cell phone priority over people you're with? Do you watch television with your cell phone? Eat with your cell phone?

Per the Pew Research Center, the cell phone is the "most quickly adopted consumer technology in the history of the world," with 91 percent of adults owning cell phones as of 2013.[37] I can only imagine we are inching closer to 100 percent as cell phones become more affordable and, frankly, necessary. People need cell phones because other people use them. The more people there are who use them, the more people will need them. Another Pew study found that "nearly two-thirds of Americans are now smartphone owners, and for many these devices are the key entry point to the online world."[38] This is not a trend I see changing.

Hooked

Perhaps as you read these possible points of addiction, you identified at least one that is, or several that are, problematic for you. Perhaps the thing that has grabbed you and refuses to let you go isn't listed. You may not have found that thing, but I believe you can recognize the patterns of addiction in the examples provided. My hope is that giving you this variety of possibilities will act as a substantial shove to push you over any stubborn hurdles of denial. I hope reading them was as personally convicting as I found it was writing them.

I have found through personal and professional experience that knowing about addictions isn't enough to avoid them. You need to know why one substance or behavior has no effect while another is a hidden trap, waiting to spring. You need to know your personal voids and which substances or behaviors you are most likely to seek to fill those voids. You need to know the ins and outs of addictions, but you also need to know the ins and outs of you.

3

Why Me?

Luis was quite proud that he grew up "taking care" of himself. His father was a functional alcoholic; at least, that's how he put it, because his father was always able to keep a job. Because his mother was so distracted managing the chaos of his father's drinking, Luis learned early on to deal with things on his own. When he was younger, he spent a great deal of time hiding out in his room, seeking to draw no attention to himself. Luis remembered sitting on the floor, in the narrow space between his bed and the wall, reading books, all the while listening intently for yelling or fighting, in case it should become directed at him. He learned to wait out those times with forced calm, though inside his gut would be tied up in knots.

Asking for what he wanted brought unwanted attention from his father or distressed paralysis from his mother. So, Luis stopped asking and discovered how to get what he needed on his own. He knew he was smart, and he learned to be clever about getting what he wanted. Taking care of his own needs, he said, came naturally.

When Initial Action Becomes Addiction

Luis told me all this in response to my questions about how his pornography addiction got started. Being of a certain age, he talked about first looking at magazines. By the time he hit his forties, print media had long since been replaced by electronic options, which provided an endless supply of Luis's "drug of choice." After his divorce, the addiction took greater hold, and his isolation from others deepened. Luis had sought help because he saw himself becoming as isolated in middle age as he had been in middle school. Luis told me he didn't want to grow old and die alone in his room.

Many factors contributed to pornography becoming his drug of choice. One such factor was an early dependence on himself and a general distrust that others would or could provide for his needs. My friend and colleague Dr. Tim Clinton would call this an attachment disorder.[1] Another was Luis's insular personality. He said he liked to be around other people but didn't need to be. With few acquaintances and no real friendships, Luis hadn't made himself accountable to anyone but himself. Yet another reason for Luis's pornography addiction was his being involved in a distant and estranged marriage for most of his life in which their one daughter received the bulk of his ex-wife's attention. He got married because she never put unreasonable demands on his time or attention. They divorced after their daughter left home and they realized they had nothing left in common.

The "why this?" and "why me?" questions of addiction usually require complex answers. An amalgamation of forces aligns to create opportunity for an action; initial action leads to adoption of the action; adoption leads to addiction. This progression to addiction is intensely individual, but there are some common threads. Family dynamics, personality traits, and genetics may help explain the roots of an addiction. Why a person ends up where they are often can be traced back to where that person started.

Family Dynamics and Survival Skills

In my work, I've come to see how childhood survival strategies can metastasize into full-grown addictions in adulthood. Some of the clearest examples have come through treating eating disorders. Eating is one of a child's earliest activities. Eating is also one of the first activities in which a child recognizes they have some level of control. A toddler turns their head to avoid the unwanted spoonful. Clamps down on the lips. Flings the rejected item across the room. Or through gesture, sound, or touch persistently communicates what is wanted. A child learns what the caregiver wants and recognizes they can cooperate—or not. Mealtimes for parents of toddlers can present a myriad of challenges in a mismatched contest of wills. In a full-circle sort of way, so can potty training, which is another basic bodily function that children learn they can, in some measure, control and use to control the adults around them.

Children are highly inventive in figuring out how to get their needs met. They learn how to manipulate their surroundings—and the people in them. Because these survival strategies are, at least somewhat, effective, the child can become conditioned to rely on and utilize them exclusively. The child who learns to whine to get what they want can become a demanding adult. The child who learns they get attention if they refuse to cooperate can become a querulous adult. The child whose caregivers aren't reliable can learn, like Luis, to rely solely on themselves.

I believe addiction can manifest in adolescence and adulthood when basic needs are unmet in childhood. The child latches on to a substance or behavior that makes the pain go away, at least for a while. That pain could be physical, like hunger, or psychological, like fear or anger. The child is concerned with relief in the moment and does not have the capacity to comprehend the long-term consequences. A major difficulty with childhood strategies, then, is they can be based on an incomplete understanding of their marginal effectiveness.

Children also watch and learn how others meet their needs. A woman I worked with was addicted to anger, which was her immediate and preferred response to just about every situation. We figured out Sheila had learned this strategy from watching her mother. Growing up, she told me, she was a constant target of her mother's displeasure. Sheila learned to feel relief, and even pleasure, when her mother's sights were turned on someone or something else. In those instances, Sheila aligned herself with her mother, attempting to avoid being a target. These times also allowed an alternative way to vent her own anger. If Shelia joined her anger to her mother's, that was acceptable. Any other expression of anger was not. As she grew, Sheila got better at mimicking her mother's anger. As she grew older still, Sheila realized how she could use her own anger to control others, just like her mother did.

I asked Sheila why she hadn't rejected her mother's anger model. Her response was simple: it was effective. Pushing back on that perspective, I brought up the damage her anger had caused in relationships. I suggested her anger was only effective in making her feel better in the short term but was, in fact, ineffective in making her relationships better in the long term. I also asked Sheila to consider the quality of her relationship with her mother now. Sheila reluctantly admitted, "I'm still afraid of her."

The Downside of Upbringing

Sheila's anger habits were so ingrained that helping her learn how to handle her anger differently was neither quick nor easy. We tried a variety of strategies and tools, with only moderate success. Waiting before speaking gave Sheila additional time to gather her ammunition. Writing letters to different people seemed to make Sheila feel worse because they codified her position.

Strangely, what worked was a peculiar visual. I told Sheila she was as addicted to her anger as her brother was to smoking, something she referred to as "a dirty and disgusting habit." I suggested every time Sheila felt herself falling into that pattern of reactive anger, she should see herself pulling out a cigarette and lighting up. I said her verbal outbursts and caustic commentaries were as self-soothing to her as a drag on a cigarette was to her brother. Why, I asked her, was his habit any more "dirty and disgusting" than hers?

Your upbringing leaves its mark—positive, negative, or both. What was your home life like? Were your needs often neglected? Did you grow up in an unstable household of unpredictability? Did you have a sense you were loved, no matter what, or did love seem inconsistent? Did you grow up afraid, discouraged, or forbidden to bring friends home? Did you have unwritten rules in your family—to hide your feelings, to keep the secrets?

Your family and your upbringing have shaped how you deal with life. Are you a second-generation venter? Are you a third-generation withdrawer? What habits have you picked up along the way? What substances or behaviors are your go-to ways of self-soothing? What did you learn back then that's giving you trouble right now? What patterns are you seeing in your life? Do they produce positive or negative results? As I've heard said, "An odd reaction is an old reaction."

As you work on these realizations, please don't allow blame to overshadow your efforts. The child who learns to handle their own needs because those around them can't or won't is not responsible. The adult, upon recognizing the negative implications of that behavior, becomes responsible to bring about positive change. The goal is not to blame the child; the goal is to empower the adult.

Personality Traits

When coming up with the answers for "why this?" and "why me?" I believe in the importance of knowing your family background, how you were raised, and the examples of behavior you saw modeled growing up. I also believe in the importance of understanding the role of personality in the formation of addictions. How you were raised may give you a higher propensity to engage in addictive behavior, but I have always suspected that your personality helps steer you toward certain types of addictions. I have come to this conclusion, again, through my work with those who have eating disorders.

Eating disorders, as I said before, incorporate the use of food to self-soothe. Anorexics restrict, bulimics binge and purge, binge eaters and night eaters binge but don't purge. Anorexics, in my experience, tend to display higher percentages of obsessive-compulsive personality traits than people in general. They can create elaborate rituals for how, when, and what they eat. They also tend to be more rigidly perfectionistic, interpreting immutable genetic traits as unacceptable and open to forced modification. I've found anorexics also carry on an almost perpetual negative self-dialogue of anxieties, fears, worries, doubts, frustrations, anger, and dissatisfaction with themselves, others, and life in general.

I have found that those who are bulimic or who compulsively overeat tend to be highly sensitive to any level of distress, with food being their immediate "medication." Their moods can swing from one extreme to the other, leading to a loss of perspective and increased impulsivity. Deep shame accompanies these eating behaviors, fueling a desire to maintain secrecy from others. They also display a greater tendency to believe in their own worthlessness and are terrified others will abandon them.

I've seen more research over the years about the role of personality traits in substance abuse than I have in behavioral or process addictions. For example, some of the personality traits associated with substance abuse have been identified as impulsivity, lack of restraint, lower regard for social conventions, poor risk assessment, manipulative tendencies, and sensation-seeking.[2]

None of these personality traits are set in stone, of course. Yet it's helpful to understand if you're a person who is especially susceptible to impulsivity, moodiness, or perfectionism. I believe in the necessity of really knowing yourself—how you "jump" in certain situations or, to use a computer term, what your "default" setting is. Once you understand which way you're more likely to jump, given your personality, you can learn skills to help you choose a different direction.

The Role of Genetics

Julia thought she was coming home to dinner. Instead, when she came in the kitchen, there sat half a dozen liquor bottles waiting for her on the kitchen counter. He'd found all of them except for the one she had hidden in the trunk of her car. He didn't say a word; he just stood there with his arms crossed. What could she say? The indictment was laid out before her and the shame was overwhelming. Julia was determined those liquor bottles had to be off the counter and out of the kitchen before their daughter walked in from practice. Avoiding his eyes, she picked up each bottle and dumped the contents into the sink while the faucet ran full strength. Julia knew they'd talk about it later, just as she knew she still had the one bottle in the car.

Like some people I've worked with over the years, Julia didn't start the road to recovery at that moment. Instead, her addiction continued for several more years until her daughter was a junior in college. Julia started on the road to recovery not for herself and not for her husband, though he'd asked her to stop in numerous ways over the years. Instead, the moment of decision came when Julia realized their daughter was following in her footsteps, and in her father's, and in his father's before that. Julia determined alcoholism was not going to take the fourth generation of her family. Have you been told you react to surprises just like your mother? Or you approach a problem like your father? Have you been told you act exactly like a grandparent who died before you were born? Do you find you have more in common with your aunt than your sister? Are you told you have your mother's eyes or your father's chin? The interplay of genetics determines your physical makeup, but researchers are also finding that genetics plays an important role in your risk for addiction. According to information from the National Institute on Drug Abuse, "Family studies that include identical twins, fraternal twins, adoptees, and siblings suggest that as much as half of a person's risk for becoming addicted to nicotine, alcohol, or other drugs depends on his or her genetic makeup."[3] Please note that the operative word here is *risk*, not *surety*.

Some people's genetic makeup causes them to be at a higher risk for cancer or Parkinson's disease or sickle-cell anemia. This doesn't mean those people will automatically contract these diseases, but they do have a greater chance of doing so. By understanding this increased risk, they can become proactive about adopting lifestyle and behavioral changes to moderate those risks. I believe the same can certainly be true for genetic predispositions toward addiction.

Understanding the Brain

In 2014, a study through the University of Texas published in *Molecular Psychiatry* found a genetic link to alcoholism.[4] Dr. R. Adron Harris, one of the authors of the study, said, "We now have a much clearer picture of where specific traits related to alcohol dependence overlap with specific expressions in the genetic code."[5] The results of this research can go both ways. Just a few years earlier, in 2010, researchers from the University of North Carolina at Chapel Hill School of Medicine found a genetic component that might protect against becoming an alcoholic.[6]

While research has been ongoing regarding how the brain reacts to addictions to substances, such as alcohol and drugs, research has also been conducted on how the brain reacts to behavioral, or process, addictions. Addictions of all kinds affect the brain's supply and utilization of neurotransmitters, such as dopamine. Dopamine, the brain's feel-good chemical, is released in what has been called the brain's pleasure center—the nucleus accumbens. That's about as technical as I can get, not being a medical professional, but as an addiction professional, I know that endorphins, such as dopamine, are a reason why addictions are so powerfully compelling.

The science of addiction has been progressing for many years and has contributed greatly to the understanding and treatment of addictions. In 1991, a scientific breakthrough took place called functional Magnetic Resonance Imaging (fMRI). Magnetic Resonance Imaging had been around since the late 1970s and used in the medical field as an alternative to traditional X-ray technology, producing different results and without its radiation implications. At the time, MRIs were confined primarily to physiological applications. However, in 1991, fMRI technology opened the human brain to exploration, exciting not only medical professionals but also psychological professionals. It became a vehicle for harnessing MRI technology by using changes in blood flow to map brain activity. So fMRI joined PET (Positron Emission Tomography) technology as a brain mapping strategy, without the need for introducing radioactive glucose into the body to act as a tracer.

I mention all of this because both PET and fMRI technology have been instrumental in tracking how the brain responds to stimuli, including the release of endorphin neurotransmitters, such as dopamine. With PET and fMRI, people like me could finally see the brain's pleasure center "light up" in response to addictive and pleasurable activities. Such technologies have allowed an even greater coordination between medical and mental health professionals in the treatment of addictive disorders.

As the understanding of addictive mechanisms has evolved, so has the accepted definition of addiction. According to the American Society of Addiction Medicine, "Addiction is a primary, chronic and relapsing brain disease characterized by an individual pathologically pursuing reward and/or relief by substance use and other behaviors."[7] Addiction is a complex web of factors that must be untangled and addressed individually to produce long-term and effective recovery.

Understanding the factors that influence your susceptibility to addiction and to specific addictive substances or behaviors is beneficial. Forewarned, as they say, is forearmed. You are, however, more than the product of your family upbringing. You have more models for living available to you as an adult than just what you saw growing up. Your personality may push you in a certain direction, but you can learn how to push back and choose a different path. Knowing your genetic risk factors for addiction can help you develop a plan to minimize those risks and provide insight into and understanding about how to avoid addictive traps in the future. Recognizing the power of addiction to rewire your neural responses gives context to the compulsion and a path forward to freedom.

4

Why Can't I Just Learn to Live with This?

Addictions mimic the cycle of an abusive relationship, with addiction acting as the perpetrator and the person becoming the victim. In a cycle of domestic violence, for example, there is a time without physical violence but when tension toward that outburst is building. The perpetrator escalates negativity and demands while the victim feels the need to control the situation by attempting to placate the perpetrator. When this strategy is ultimately unsuccessful, the perpetrator begins to abuse, blaming the victim, who feels helpless to resist. After the perpetrator acts out against the victim, both perpetrator and victim feel a sense of relief. The perpetrator often apologizes, gives gifts, and promises to change while the victim minimizes the abuse, leading to a period of calm that can last varying amounts of time—anywhere from hours to days to weeks. What is certain is the eventual return of the tension and subsequent abuse. I've seen this cycle repeated in the case of addiction.

I used this analogy with someone I was working with who had come to me after leaving an abusive marriage. Mary left that relationship but struggled with ongoing depression. Her depression, I soon diagnosed, was complicated by an entrenched eating disorder that erupted after her divorce. Mary was convinced all she needed was help to "get back on track." When I explained her eating disorder, Mary was resistant to change. She minimized her behavior, telling me she needed those foods to cope with her depression.

Her eating disorder, I suggested, was creating another cycle of abuse. Instead of a person starting the abusive cycle, I proposed it was her eating disorder that kept up the litany of negativity and demands. Invariably, Mary would give in to those demands through a pattern of nighttime bingeing on sweet and salty foods. After each binge, she experienced a relief period, and her eating disorder would stay quiet for a while. The relief, however, never lasted, and within a few days or maybe a week, as Mary became more and more depressed, she would be back in the cycle.

Because I believed her depression and her eating disorder were linked, I insisted we needed to work on both. The solution, Mary felt, was information and education about how to eat better. I agreed this would be helpful and scheduled her with our medical and nutritional staff. Within these sessions, however, Mary was resistant to making dietary and nutritional changes. Hearing about them was one thing; doing them, she found, was something altogether different.

Mary argued against the idea that eating was contributing so directly to her depression. After her divorce, food became her new relationship. It provided surety, comfort, and stress relief, and Mary had great difficulty recognizing that relationship as addictive and, more, as abusive. Frankly, she didn't want to give up her unhealthy relationship with food. Instead, Mary wanted to find ways to keep her eating disorder "under control."

Addictions, like abusive relationships, cannot be kept under control. Addictions, like abusers, take control, no matter what they say in the "honeymoon" phase of apologies and promises. Addictions, like abusers, will say whatever is necessary to continue the behavior. They are concerned only with their goals and their gratification, regardless of the victim. Excuses, protestations of change, and elaborate rationales are given to victims for one reason only—to perpetuate the behavior.

Upside-Down Thinking

When speaking about those I've worked with to overcome addiction, I said in the introduction that some loved their addiction and viewed it as an engaging but unruly child. They wanted me to help them manage their addiction so they could hold on to it. Mary was in that category. Because of the abuse she'd suffered in her marriage, Mary couldn't see the depth of damage from her eating disorder.

Stepping away from her abusive marriage was incredibly traumatic, and Mary had shown immense courage in doing what she had to do to keep herself safe. I challenged her to use what she'd learned during that time to help her overcome and recover this time. This time, however, another person wasn't involved. Instead, Mary was acting as both perpetrator and victim. Having overcome an abusive relationship, she found it difficult to see her relationship with food as abusive. Initially, all Mary could see was what she called the "positives": she was no longer being belittled and beaten, what she ate was her choice and no one else's, and gaining weight was no longer a big deal because she didn't plan on becoming involved in another relationship.

Over the course of several months, I carefully proposed that none of those "positives" were true. Mary was still being belittled by the eating disorder, and every time she gave in, she felt beaten. What she ate was no longer her choice; it was dictated by her eating disorder. Gaining weight was a big deal because of the health risks involved. And Mary was in another relationship—this time with food. This addictive relationship with food was directly contributing to her ongoing depression.

People who cling to their addictions often have this upside-down type of thinking. They see the addiction not as net-harmful but as net-beneficial. I cannot tell you how many times I have heard people make excuses for the damaging consequences of their addiction by protesting that, without it, things would have been "so much worse."

I understand that sentiment, because I felt it myself as I struggled to come to grips with my workaholism. When I started seeing how destructive those work habits were, my first thought was to focus on all the "disasters" that overworking might have avoided. I justified my behavior with a supply of dramatic "what-ifs." What if I hadn't put in those hours? What if I hadn't sacrificed what I did to grow my business? What if I wasn't as successful? My perceived positives were powerful enough at first to overcome the true negatives.

But there comes a point in addictive behavior when the balance shifts and you start to realize there aren't as many "positives" as you had thought. As Mary began to recognize the true nature of her eating disorder, she had trouble reconciling being both the perpetrator and the victim. To avoid blaming herself as the former while empathizing with herself as the latter, Mary did what others have done—she separated the two. She began to refer to the voice in her head, this compulsion to fill her voids with food, as "ED" for Eating Disorder. No, her ex-husband wasn't named Ed, but using a male name helped her create distance from the behavior. She and others have referred to their eating-disorder behaviors as ED. My friend Cynthia Rowland McClure called her bulimia "The Monster Within."[1]

You may not have a name for your behavior, but do you sometimes think fondly of your addiction? Do you find yourself feeling grateful for the positives you feel, regardless of how negative your addiction has become? Is your addiction jealous of those positives? Does it tell you that only by engaging in the addiction can you feel safe, comforted, validated, empowered, or free? What is that voice in your head telling you to compel you to act in certain ways? Yes, that's your own voice, but does it carry the subtle, or not-so-subtle, undertones of someone else?

Your addiction isn't your friend; it's not your lover; it's not the thing that knows you best; it's not the thing that saves you from disaster; it's not the thing you can't live without. These are all examples of the upside-down thinking of addiction. Addiction first tries to convince you how inseparable you are from your addiction—how much you need it, with all its false positives. Addiction then grabs a seat of priority through this upside-down thinking and savagely holds to that place. Addiction will not voluntarily step down; only you can knock it off its perch.

Destructive Thinking

I also said in the introduction that some people dealing with an addiction hated their addiction and wanted to find a way to destroy it without destroying themselves in the process. There is a danger when a person comes to understand how terrible their addiction is. That danger is self-loathing. They come to hate the addiction so much, they risk hating themselves in the process.

Eric grew up going to church, so he knew how bad he was. He'd already blown half a dozen commandments in his mind. God, Eric concluded, couldn't forgive him, so why should he go to all this trouble to change if it was of no use? Eric was convinced he could never undo the damage he'd already done. When we talked about this, Eric said he was like Judas. The only path left was to hang himself, though he said that remark was metaphorical when I called him on it. By hanging himself, Eric clarified he meant continuing in the addiction.

Some people are drawn to their addiction; they want it to continue. Some are repelled by their addiction; they don't want it to continue, but they see no way for that to happen without ceasing to "continue" themselves. Yet the power of self-preservation is strong. They do continue, resigning themselves to the "fact" that "it's too late" or "there's no use" or "what's the point?" As they look over the edge of that hopeless abyss, a wishful part of them wants to know if there's a way to destroy the addiction without having to destroy themselves. A pessimistic part also says there isn't a way and the only way to continue is to learn to live with whatever it is.

Addiction throws up a barrage of false positives when confronted with a person's desire to change. Addiction can also throw up a barrage of false negatives, making it seem like giving up the addiction means losing parts of yourself. Addiction infiltrates a person's identity and sense of self, making it hard to tell one from the other. Have you ever had a weed in your yard that closely resembled a legitimate plant? You're afraid of pulling up the one for fear you'll destroy the other. Addiction can mimic you to avoid getting uprooted by speaking through your voice and with your thoughts so it's hard for you to tell the difference. When you become so intertwined with your addiction, contemplating ending it can seem like a form of figurative suicide.

Resolve Erosion

The goal of an addiction is to continue. When confronted with "never again," an addiction is going to find a way to turn that into "just once more." Again and again and again. A thirteen-year-old who starts to drink has no concept of what decades of alcohol will mean. A fifteen-year-old who vomits to lose weight has no concept of what decades of purging will do to their body. A twenty-one-year-old who wagers bets has no concept of how decades of gambling will affect their life. With an addiction, the end of a matter is never revealed. Instead, the addiction concentrates solely on the short term.

If it takes becoming your best friend so you'll never think of changing, so be it. If it takes becoming your worst enemy so you'll never believe you could change, so be it. An addiction wants you to learn to live with it—as a friend or a foe or anything in between.

Where are you on this spectrum of friend or foe? Does your addiction change from moment to moment or day to day? Has it changed over the span of the addiction, starting out as one thing and morphing into another? Where is your addiction now?

Vanishing Return

Finally, I said some people I have worked with wanted to end the addiction but felt lost and no longer knew who they were. They were afraid that once the addiction was gone, they would cease to exist as well. This was the issue with a woman I worked with whose children had done a type of intervention to convince her to go into treatment.

Teresa's addiction was not to food or alcohol but to her relationships with her children. She was terrified they would at some point abandon her. Truthfully, after speaking with two of her three children during our admissions process, that was a real possibility. They spoke of the manipulative phone calls, the unreasonable demands, the poisonous guilt Teresa used with them. They were adults now, with families of their own, and were at the point of cutting off the relationship. They spoke about needing to breathe;

they felt strangled by her. One of them said their mother was like a drowning person; to save herself, she kept forcing them under.

I believe you face a greater danger of losing your sense of identity to an addiction if you had little or no sense of identity before the addiction. If you do not have a clear sense of self, an addiction has a wide-open field to take over, with no real obstacle in its way. If you saw yourself before your addiction as a person with no real significance, without the addiction, you return to insignificance. Who will you be then? How will you cope? Isn't it better to find a way to keep what little you've got?

The problem with an addiction is that the little keeps shrinking. It certainly threatened to in Teresa's case. Without a change, she was about to lose her relationships with her adult children and, by extension, her young grandchildren. The very thing Teresa feared—being rejected by her children—was about to happen. The tighter Teresa hung on to those relationships, the more they were slipping away.

Addiction wants to convince you of one thing—it is all you have. Addiction is loath to reveal any other alternatives for filling your needs, lest you change your behavior. When you begin to see your addiction as ruining your life, the addiction may start to negotiate. You may hear all the false positives of staying in the relationship. When those are no longer as effective, you may start to hear the false negatives of breaking away, including the loss of who you think you are.

Mary came to understand that ED was an abusive relationship and not a way to avoid her pain. Eric came to a place where he could both acknowledge the damage of his addiction and still have room to forgive himself. Teresa found when her relationship with herself was stronger, she could loosen her grip on her relationships with others. All of them came to understand addiction lies when it says you can learn to live with it. There is no living *with* an addiction; there is only living *for* an addiction.

5

Who Am I without This?

Once you give up on the idea of a future where your addiction is "manageable," you must contemplate a future without the addiction in any form. The question then becomes, "Who am I without this?" The addiction has been such an integral part of your life that you have difficulty imagining what life could be, who you could be, without it.

This point was brought home to me last year. I was working with a woman who was trying to overcome a prescription drug addiction. Amy was in the phase of recovery where she was ready to accept the negatives of her addiction but fearful of what life would mean without it. During this time, she got a card from an old friend. She said they'd drifted apart because they no longer lived in the same state. Their correspondences, Amy told me, were usually a yearly holiday missive giving a personal and family update. The midyear card came as a surprise and contained a picture of the two of them that was more than thirty years old. Amy showed me the candid shot of a group of teenagers and asked if I could pick her out.

As I struggled to avoid embarrassment by choosing the wrong person, Amy said it was a picture of her church youth group getting ready to take off for a day hike. When I didn't pick her out right away, she gratefully let me off the hook and pointed herself out. She lamented how far she'd come from that young, smiling teenage girl. "I can't remember who I was," Amy said, "and if I give this up, I can't imagine who I'll be."

I believe this question of who you'll be without your addiction is a common one. Addiction has the power to co-opt the person you are and change you into someone different, altering your thoughts, actions, and behaviors. The person you were becomes a faded, distant memory. You may look in a mirror and feel unsure of who you were, ashamed of who you are, and fearful of becoming anyone else.

I think people are fearful of giving up an addiction because they believe they will be in pain without it. I've heard this sentiment expressed in different ways, though rarely will they use the word *pain*. Instead, they say without their addiction, they will be frustrated or bored, anxious or afraid. They tell me the addiction, whatever it is, helps them overcome being depressed or angry. In the deepest throes of my overworking, my pain might have carried the name *unsuccessful* or *failure*.

Altered Reality

Addiction has the power to mask the "real" self, the pain-filled self, by providing a veneer of concealment. Within this altered reality, people believe the addiction keeps the pain at bay. When asked to look in the mirror without the mask of addiction, they're afraid all they will see is pain.

Larry's friends and family were desperate for him to overcome his alcoholism, which they'd watched take hold over several years.

Larry was less convinced of the need to change, as drinking had become his shield against a host of adversaries, including himself. Alcohol was his way to tolerate social situations, where he felt especially vulnerable. Alcohol meant first relief, then numbness, and finally forgetfulness. Alcohol shut down the negative voice in his head, or at least caused him not to remember what it said.

Drinking held back the emotional pain Larry had felt for as long as he could remember, allowing him to enter an altered state of temporary relief. To him, that seemed an acceptable trade-off. As Larry warmed to the subject of why he didn't want to stop drinking, he told me about the physical pain. He said he'd tried to quit on his own several times but was thwarted by the mental confusion and extreme discomfort of his cold-turkey approach. Drinking, he said, might not be that good for him, but without it, Larry assured me, he was a mess.

That's when I shared the letters from his family and good friends. They spoke about the person Larry became when he drank, someone they were fearful of and ashamed for. They detailed the ways he'd used their friendship only to keep drinking. One friend wrote about the times Larry had turned up on his doorstep, drunk, incoherent, and stinking of vomit and urine. Larry thought he'd be a mess without drinking; his friend reminded him of the times he was a mess because of drinking.

I've known people who thought they were hysterically funny, intellectually witty, or sexually desirable while under the influence of drugs or alcohol, when quite the opposite was true. I've known those with an eating disorder who considered their skeletal frames the epitome of attractiveness while other people felt shock and horror upon seeing their malnourished bodies. I've known people addicted to their anger who thought people viewed them as decisive and strong. I've known people addicted to their work who thought they were providing for their families, when in truth, they were losing them. Their addiction altered their sense of reality.

Obscured by the mask of their addiction, they could no longer see themselves for who they were. Alcohol, drugs, eating disorders, or other addictions allow people to imagine they are stronger, smarter, sexier, more popular, or less vulnerable than they really are.

Virtual Masks

In an odd way, with the advent of the internet, I've watched these addictive "masks" that people wear take on virtual shape. The internet acts as a breeding ground for artificially created personas, shaped by the altered reality of addiction. On social media, a person can give a face and a narrative to their altered reality. Is it any wonder there are people who have become addicted to Facebook, social media, and their smartphones? Who feel compelled to constantly monitor their online presence, to make sure the "mask" doesn't slip?

Is it any wonder, then, the power of something like online gaming, where an altered reality can become a supercharged avatar operating within a virtual world? Online gaming allows people to not only create new identities but also spend a significant portion of their lives subsumed by them. With the creativity of online gaming, you can customize these personas to look as much—or as little—like you as you want. Gamers speak about the draw of the freedom within their created avatars to become either more like who they think they are or the opposite of who they're afraid they are.

Hasn't that always been a hallmark of an addiction—the ability to transport yourself into an alternate reality, allowing you to escape a painful truth? All sorts of substances and activities can provide the conduit for such desperate imagination. When imagination and alternate realities are stripped away, all that is left are those painful truths. This generation now has a wider choice of options, of places to hide.

Because I am of a certain age with teenagers of my own and because of my profession, distressed parents tend to find me. In the past, because of my work with those who have eating disorders, there seemed to be mostly parents of girls and young women pulling me aside and speaking in hushed tones. However, in the past several years, because of recent books concerning boys and technology, parents of boys and young men are balancing out the ratio.

I met with the parents of a twenty-year-old who were distressed about what was happening to their son. Things seemed fine throughout high school, but after graduation, his mother said, Michael didn't seem to be making much of a life for himself. His father, at this point, interrupted and said Michael was making quite a life for himself—but on video games. They still had high hopes for Michael's post-secondary education but pulled him out of school because of dismal grades. All he wanted to do, they told me, was play games on the computer. They were alternately concerned, angry, frustrated, and fearful about his seeming lack of ambition. His only motivation appeared to be singularly directed toward what Michael's father called "a useless activity."

When I met with Michael, however, he considered his online gaming to be anything but useless. On the contrary, Michael squarely saw the "life" his parents wanted for him fall under the useless category. Their vision of his future and Michael's own were significantly at odds. High school was over and the point of divergence between his plans and theirs could no longer be avoided. The stress of that schism was sending Michael running to the alternate reality of his addiction—video games. Real life contained all the stress of failure, disappointment, tension, and strife between him and his parents. Increasingly, he found himself slipping into the virtual world, where he had control over his persona and, more importantly, his battles. Leaving behind his artificially created reality meant confronting a particularly painful time in his life. Leaving behind his avatars meant facing the world

75

only as himself. And Michael was terrified of being inadequate, unable to live up to his parents' expectations and his own.

As I listened to Michael agonize over the difficulty of living life unmasked, as it were, I realized how true that was for others dealing with addictions. Addictions become an acceptable alternative when real life is littered with doubts, fears, worries, frustrations, anger, and bitterness. The addiction helps you create a type of avatar that allows you to become someone who seems less vulnerable to pain. The truth is that the addiction doesn't take away pain; it adds to your pain, tricking you into believing you need it even more.

As I worked with him, Michael admitted he was afraid of becoming "one of those guys" who spent their productive years living in their parents' basement. However, he was afraid of disappointing his parents by not being as successful going forward as either his parents or he wanted. I suggested he needed to alter not his reality but his standard for success. I also suggested the only way to really test himself was to get up off the couch and get into the real world.

Addictions are not the real world. They create artificial avatars that promise to fight your battles and shield your pain. They promise to hype your attributes and pump up your skills and abilities. They promise to make you more than you are without them. In truth, however, they do the opposite. They create more battles than they resolve; they produce more pain than they shield. They downgrade your attributes and degrade your skills and abilities. You become less and less with them than you could be without them, losing your sense of reality and identity. When an addiction becomes your identity, you can have difficulty knowing who you are anymore.

Who are you without your addiction? Does a part of you believe you're stronger, smarter, sexier, or better somehow with your addiction than without it? Are you worried you're so tied to your addictive identity that you won't have an identity without it? Are you afraid that without your addiction all you will be in is pain? What about the pain you're in now?

Seeing herself in that thirty-year-old picture was an eye-opener for Amy. When she looked back at who she was, she didn't recognize herself. Slowly, however, she became reacquainted with that young teenager. Amy knew she had a life before the addiction, which helped her to realize life was possible after the addiction. Amy wasn't ready to answer "Who am I without it?" but she was at least ready to consider the answer could be more than "in pain."

6

Why Can't I See What This Is Doing to Me?

One thing I've learned over the years is that addiction blinds people to the truth of consequences. Addiction causes people to misinterpret these negative impacts across a wide spectrum, including emotional consequences, intellectual consequences, physical consequences, and spiritual consequences. Because we treat the whole person at The Center, we see and work with these multiple impacts daily.

Emotional Consequences

Brandon came to us professing to feel nothing. When Brandon was asked in group sessions how he felt about a story or concept, his stock response was to shrug and say, "I don't know." If asked to describe how he felt about a memory he shared, he would seem puzzled by the question. As we worked with Brandon, we soon suspected that when he said, "I don't know," he desperately was trying to achieve "I don't care." Brandon did care; he cared deeply. But caring, he'd learned, made you vulnerable and susceptible to pain.

I've found, for some people, addictions can act as emotional dams, holding back pain. The addictive behaviors create a structure behind which disturbing emotions are kept contained. The illusion is these emotions are being kept under control, but that is not the case. The floodwaters of pain continue to build and apply tremendous pressure to the structure of the addiction, requiring continual fortification.

Because of the perceived danger of any sort of release, these emotional dams hold back pleasure as well as pain. Happiness, gratitude, interest, empathy, desire, and delight are walled off too. In my line of work, a person who is emotionally damming is said to have a flat affect. The blank face of their emotional dam is, quite literally, their own face, which displays little or no emotion. That was certainly true in Brandon's case.

Emotional content being held back will continue its destructive pressure unless that pressure is released. In an odd way, one of our jobs at The Center is to burst emotional dams. We act as professional spillways, allowing that pent-up emotional pressure to be expressed within a supportive environment.

Breakdown or Breakthrough

Tears, therefore, in my business, can be incredibly cleansing. When Brandon finally broke, he did so with a torrent of tears. He kept apologizing, choking out that he couldn't stop crying, as if that was somehow unacceptable. He seemed genuinely shocked at the intensity of what he called his "breakdown." I suggested he jettison the word *breakdown* and consider his experience a breakthrough. Weathering that flood of emotion was difficult, but it allowed him to begin the slow process of learning how to "feel" again—apart from the emotional suffocation of his addiction.

Some people come to us suppressing all emotions, and they are a challenge to open. Others are just the opposite. They are a challenge to contain because they scatter their emotional states, which are almost always negative, indiscriminately in every conceivable direction. I've had my manhood impugned, my professionalism vilified, and my Christianity called into question. I've been yelled at, cussed at, cried over, raged against, argued with, bargained with, and accused of every nefarious motive possible amid these emotional tempests.

Emotional Deregulation

Morgan came to The Center in full-blown crisis mode. Everything was a problem, an issue, a catastrophe ripe for response. If required to wait for help at our welcome desk, Morgan was sure she was being marginalized. If asked to refrain from some distracting habit in group sessions, she was being punished. If obligated to adhere to direction, she was being unfairly coerced. Morgan had no off switch, not even a dimmer switch. Her emotions were full-on, all the time. The staff, quite frankly, found dealing with her exhausting. In empathy, though, we knew Morgan found dealing with herself even more so, which was why she routinely abused whatever pharmaceuticals she had convinced previous physicians to prescribe.

Addiction steals from a person's capacity for emotional regulation, the capacity to consciously choose how to respond to an emotional reaction. Emotional regulation isn't an everyday concept, but it's an everyday occurrence. We learn from our upbringing and experience how to respond to emotional reactions. We watch how others respond, and we watch what happens when they do.

Brandon's upbringing taught him that emotional responses brought punishment. He learned dismay was unacceptable, childlike delight and joy were excessive, any show of pride was unbecoming,

81

and anger was flat-out rebellious. Brandon grew up not being allowed to express what he felt. But holding so much emotion inside was painful, so he learned it was better to feel nothing at all.

Morgan's upbringing taught her that her emotional responses brought adult attention. When Morgan expressed negative emotions, she was cuddled, coddled, and shielded from that negativity. Yet when she expressed positive emotions, anything positive was immediately whisked away by others. She wasn't allowed to keep what she felt, so she learned to feel everything as immediately and extremely as possible. His was an emotional drought, hers an emotional flood. Emotional regulation supplies a middle ground between a Goldilocks conundrum of not enough emotion on the one hand and too much on the other.

Intellectual Consequences

I've always thought of intelligence as mental capacity, which can change over a person's lifetime. I do believe a person is born with a certain innate intellectual capacity, but I also believe a variety of factors play into mental capacity, such as experience and opportunity. In addition, physical factors, such as injury or disease, can interfere with mental capacity.

Intelligence isn't my professional field, but I've seen how addiction can have an impact on a person's mental capacity. Alex came in for depression after attending his twentieth high school reunion. He understood that people tend to put their best foot forward at these kinds of events, but still, Alex said he was disheartened by what he saw. When I asked specifically what that was, he talked about how much further along other people were in their lives. I asked Alex what he was measuring, and he mentioned families, kids, careers, a sense of accomplishment, and an optimism about the future. He said he felt he didn't have as much to show for the time he'd been on the earth. Alex said he left the reunion in a state of deep depression that he hadn't been able to shake.

It took a while to unpack why Alex thought his life required some sort of production schedule. Through that process, though, he revealed he had started smoking pot in high school. He was quick to point out that he had never "graduated" to "hard drugs" and had just stayed with pot. I asked him what effects he thought his marijuana use had on his life. He started by mentioning the benefits—specifically the relaxation it afforded him. He also said he was glad he lived in a state where it wasn't illegal to use anymore, as that had made his life easier.

I asked Alex what he thought the negative impacts were. I expected something along the lines of health issues related to smoking or possible legal implications of driving or possession. Instead, Alex said he thought he'd "settled" for pot too often in his life. If something was difficult or uncomfortable, he chose to smoke pot. He said he got used to being comfortable and, subsequently, had lost his "edge."

Scientific discussions about the ramifications of long-term marijuana use aside, I thought Alex's answers were intriguing and applicable to a variety of addictions. I thought of those with eating disorders who spend years revolving their lives around their relationship with food. Addictions take time, energy, and attention away from other pursuits, including the types of experiences and opportunities that can have a positive impact on mental capacity. Addictions can dull insight, highjack inspiration, sidetrack creativity, and squash curiosity. Addictions can reduce a kaleidoscope of possibilities down to a solitary addictive lens.

I suggested Alex was just out of practice with the types of experiences that stretch a person. He was under forty years old, and I assured him life wasn't over. He reluctantly agreed to an evaluation and entered our substance use program. Giving up pot wasn't easy, but over time he began to reinvigorate his sense of the possible and reactivate his stagnant intellectual drive. Again, I haven't found this intellectual stagnation to be unique to one addiction. I've seen people recover from addictions of all kinds and go back to school, change careers, establish new careers, and refresh existing commitments with increased concentration and vigor. Addiction doesn't want that to happen. It wants to extinguish the spark of determination and discovery, as it is jealous and resentful of being crowded out by positive things.

Physical Consequences

Some people may operate under the mistaken notion that the only addictions with negative physical impacts are those dealing with drugs or alcohol. That is not the case. Any addiction, whether fueled by a substance or a behavior, has the potential to negatively impact a person's physical health. At The Center, we've addressed those physical concerns for more than thirty years.

One hurdle of denial that people have trouble navigating deals with these negative physical impacts. Because the addiction can produce a temporary physical sensation of pleasure or reward, the addiction can be falsely perceived as physically beneficial. People find it difficult to comprehend the long-term physical damage the addiction causes.

According to the National Institute on Drug Abuse (part of the National Institutes of Health), the physical impacts of substance addictions are significant. Broken down by substances, the results are sobering.

- Injecting drugs accounts for around 12 percent of new AIDS cases and contributes to the spread of communicable disease, such as hepatitis C.

- The nicotine found in tobacco products increases the risk of cancer, emphysema, bronchial disorders, and cardiovascular disease. According to their calculations, tobacco use contributed to the deaths of around one hundred million people worldwide during the last century. If that trend continues, that number may hit one billion in this century.
- Alcohol can damage body organs as well as the brain.
- Marijuana impairs short-term memory and learning as well as concentration and coordination. It increases heart rate and can harm the lungs. With the presence of other conditions, it can increase the risk of psychosis.
- Misusing certain prescription medications can lead to addiction and, in some cases, death.
- Inhalants are, generally, very toxic and can damage major organs, such as the heart, lungs, brain, and kidneys. Unlike some substances, inhalants can produce heart failure and death within a short time of a single incident of prolonged sniffing.
- Cocaine is a short-acting stimulant that leads to problems with the heart as well as the respiratory, nervous, and digestive systems.
- Amphetamines are stimulants that can produce feelings of alertness and even euphoria. They raise the body temperature and can create heart problems and seizures. Methamphetamines can be harmful to the brain.
- Ecstasy can increase body temperature, heart rate, and blood pressure and generate heart-wall stress. LSD is a potent hallucinogen, producing sensations, sights, and colors that do not exist. Heroin produces euphoria and feelings of relaxation while it slows respiration.
- Steroids can cause severe acne, heart disease, liver problems, stroke, and infectious diseases.[1]

I am all too acquainted with the physical damage to body systems done by eating disorders. I have known young anorexics with the bones of seventy-year-olds. I have known bulimics with a mouthful of rotted teeth. I have known overeaters faced with the need for hip and knee replacements.

For those with a behavioral or process addiction, I've found the single greatest physical impact is the constant stress of dealing with their addiction. The American Psychological Association lists the following stress effects on the body:

- Muscle tension
- Stress headaches and migraines
- Hyperventilation or overbreathing
- Asthma attacks
- Panic attacks
- Increased heart rate
- Elevated blood pressure
- Heart attack
- Stroke
- Inflamed coronary arteries
- Elevated cholesterol levels
- Increased stress hormone levels of adrenaline, epinephrine, and cortisol
- Increased blood glucose levels
- Acid reflux
- Stomach pain
- Ulcers
- Diarrhea or constipation
- Diminished testosterone production
- Diminished sperm production

- Erectile dysfunction
- Increased vulnerability to infection
- Premenstrual syndrome
- Increased menopausal symptoms
- Decreased sexual desire[2]

Addiction, bluntly, can damage your body, reducing quality of life and fast-forwarding the aging process. Substance addictions can bring in toxic levels from the outside, while process addictions can produce toxic levels from the inside. The body will withstand the toxic effects depending on general health and genetics, but, eventually, addiction creates a no-win situation. Because these effects have been present over time, some people do not connect their addictive behaviors to their physical challenges.

The good news is the body has a remarkable ability to heal itself when properly supported. At The Center, we bring together medical and naturopathic physicians as well as dietitians to provide such support to those recovering from addiction. We teach techniques and skills to handle and reduce stress. We seek to reacquaint people with the art of listening to their physical bodies and responding in constructive ways to repair the damage. We have seen the physical damage but have also witnessed amazing physical transformations due to the body's power to heal and respond to healthy treatment.

Spiritual Consequences

"Why hasn't God answered my prayers?" In that one question, Lauren seemed to communicate hope and despair, optimism and frustration. As a Christian counselor working with people of faith, I have always included spirituality as a component of my whole-person approach. Addiction and recovery from addiction, in my experience, touch deeply into spiritual matters. Addiction can take on a life of its own and create a sense of powerlessness in those addicted. Is it any wonder, then, that people seek out something or someone greater than themselves to help them overcome the power of their addiction?

Nowhere is this principle better demonstrated than in the Twelve Steps from Alcoholics Anonymous, so many of which speak directly to the role of spirituality, faith, and belief in God as a cornerstone to recovery.

As I said before, addiction is jealous. It does not want anything to get in the way of its power over a person. As such, addiction can create an atmosphere of shame, worthlessness, and guilt in those who are addicted. Addiction is not beyond using a person's faith as a weapon against them, telling the person they are irredeemable, unworthy of forgiveness, and doomed to condemnation. Addiction seeks to speak with a distortion of God's voice, denying faith's promise of acceptance, forgiveness, and redemption.

I asked Lauren to consider that God had, indeed, answered her prayers, as she was at The Center, in treatment, with the possibility of learning more about herself, her addiction, and the power of God to heal. I perceived she wanted a lightning strike, a bolt of faith that would come down from heaven and remove her addiction, and I asked her if that was true. Lauren considered my question for a moment and then admitted, yes, she was so tired that she just wanted God to take the addiction from her.

I had to honestly explain that through the years I'd seen such immediate and spectacular things happen, but more often I'd seen recovery happen over time, as people slowly walked step-by-step through recovery. I commented that even Christ walked a path to the cross that involved suffering and, ultimately, victory.

The theme verse of The Center, Jeremiah 29:11, says, "'For I know the plans I have for you,' declares the LORD, 'plans to prosper you and not to harm you, plans to give you hope and a future.'" People struggling with addiction desperately need to know, or to remember, that God can provide them with a hopeful future—a future without addiction. Faith, which is the confidence in what we hope for and assurance about what we do not see,[3] can act as the forward vision that sees beyond the devastation of the addiction. Without that forward vision, the landscape is littered with the wreckage of the addiction, which seems impossible to overcome.

Where is your faith? Has an addiction chipped away at it until very little is left? If that's true, have hope. Jesus said faith as small as a mustard seed can move mountains.[4]

7

Why Can't I See What This Is Doing to Others?

"I don't even know who you are anymore." I couldn't decide which was more tragic, the statement itself or the way she said it—in utter defeat. And she wasn't done. "So I don't even know who I am anymore."

There comes a point in most counseling for addiction issues when the person's support structure is brought into the process. This support structure is, generally, immediate family members, such as spouses, parents, or children, but can also include extended family and friends. The goal of these support sessions is for the person to realize they are not alone and others are willing to assist in their recovery. These sessions are not always easy because, in my experience, the addiction has universally damaged these relationships. No matter how strong, these relationships still are not whole and the brokenness needs to be acknowledged and addressed.

Lisa and Daniel had been married more than twenty years. Not quite a decade into the marriage, Daniel's gambling pastime turned into addiction. Before long, that got coupled with substance abuse. Over time, as these addictions took greater hold of Daniel's life, the threads holding together the marriage frayed. Lisa said when she'd vowed "for better or worse," she always thought at least they would be together. She hadn't been prepared for the way Daniel's addictions would force them apart.

A significant disconnect can develop during the recovery process between someone struggling with addiction and their family members or friends. I've experienced situations in which the addicted person believed it was the duty of the family member or friend to support recovery without bringing up any objections or consequences from the past. Some people have a sense that recovery is a "do-over" and whatever happened in the past should stay in the past. Because the recovery is new and the emotions are still raw, I've seen people who are reluctant to confront the past, with a mind-set that, to move forward, the past should become off-limits.

The Presence of Pain

This mind-set, however, does not account for the pain experienced by the loved one because of the addiction. That pain, while it may have happened in the past, is still very present in the mind and heart of the loved one. And that present pain may not have had any outlet for expression in the past. While the addiction was active, the addicted person was compromised and often incapable of truly recognizing the truth of the other person's pain. The crisis mentality that addiction generates leaves very little room for addressing anyone else's pain, which, put simply, gets shoved to the back burner.

However, during the recovery process, as the person's mind clears, their ability to recognize the pain of others comes into clearer focus. While the addiction was active, the sole focus of the relationship was the addiction. During the recovery process, the focus of the relationship can shift to include the feelings and perspectives of the other person. Those feelings and perspectives can be negative, centered on the frustration, anger, disappointment, and despair felt as a by-product of the addiction.

I should also mention that this pain, felt by loved ones, is not just relegated to the past or the present. Pain, in the mind of the loved one, remains a distinct possibility for the future. Often this is due to the cyclical nature of addiction recovery (which I'll discuss in depth in a later chapter). Addiction recovery is rarely a "one and done"; it takes multiple efforts to accomplish. So, often the loved one has been at this place of recovery before, only to have the person relapse. They naturally may fear that this recovery will not last and that the addiction as well as the pain it produces could resurface.

If the addicted person is in a relationship, recovery from addiction, by definition, must encompass recovery within the relationship. Because the relationship involves more than one person, the addicted person cannot solely dictate what healing will look like. The other person, who has already been marginalized by the addiction, must have the opportunity to voice their experiences, even if it's extremely uncomfortable for the recovering person to hear. They must have a voice in the path to relationship recovery.

Daniel told me listening to Lisa explain how she'd been hurt by his addiction was like being emotionally dragged over broken glass. Every sharp edge of pain she voiced cut deep into his identity as a man and a husband. He said he fought the desire to defend himself, to bring up times when she'd hurt him, to walk away so he didn't have to listen anymore. Daniel's reemerging love for Lisa, however, kept him seated and listening, as recovery in their relationship depended on this.

Collateral Damage

Why go through that pain when you're still so vulnerable? Why is relationship so important within addiction recovery? I believe addiction is, at its core, a relationship. In some ways, the relationship with the addiction becomes more intimate than with other people. A dictionary definition of *relationship* is the way in which two or more concepts, objects, or people are connected, or the state of being connected. An addict has been intimately connected to the source of their addiction. This addiction connection warps all other relationships. Those people connected to the addict—and by extension, to the addiction—become recipients of collateral damage.

Regarding immediate family members—whether spouses, parents, or children—one of the most prevalent forms of collateral damage I've heard expressed is loneliness. As the addiction consumes greater amounts of their loved one's time, energy, and attention, they find themselves crowded out, abandoned to live a life alone or to live a life subservient to the addiction—or a combination of the two. Their own needs, wants, and desires are boxed out, placed on hold. Lisa spoke in terms of abandonment, as she realized Daniel's greatest pleasures in life, his reasons for living, no longer had anything to do with her. Lisa said she felt as if she'd stopped being Daniel's partner and had been relegated to maid, cook, and an inconsequential sexual release. As difficult as it was for me as a third party to hear this brutal truth, I felt it had to be even more so for Daniel and was thankful he had allowed Lisa to speak about her pain.

Because addiction is so consuming, people in recovery have talked about coming back into the light or having blinders removed. This awakening can be joyful as they discover a renewed ability to see and experience the "real" world around them, unshrouded by the addiction. However, this awakening can also be quite painful, akin to coming out of a dark room and walking into harsh sunlight.

As I said before, these support sessions with loved ones are not easy. In fact, they can be a clinical risk. Before undertaking such a risk, I need to have some level of assurance the person is ready, is strong enough to experience such truth. If the person is not ready or has not gained enough skills to remain resilient, such revelations can end up conversely supporting their escape back into the addiction.

I remember a family support session between Tracy and her two daughters. Tracy's addiction was not to a substance but to a behavior—anger. The girls, for the first time, candidly told Tracy what growing up within her orbit was like. Clearly, even in their twenties, Kelsey and Kaitlyn were still terrified of Tracy but determined to finally speak their truth. They shared their childhood memories, of huddling in their rooms, fearful of becoming her target. They spoke about how they self-censored activities they did or things they asked for to try to preemptively avoid Tracy's caustic responses. Kelsey and Kaitlyn talked about being afraid to have friends over out of fear Tracy would humiliate them by going into one of her tirades. They mentioned feeling there was always a barrier between her and them that prevented them from seeking out the love, companionship, and comfort they so often needed from her. The girls admitted they had clung instead to each other for that support, further driving a wedge of alienation in their relationship with their mother.

When it was Tracy's turn to talk, her first comment was, "I had no idea." I was so grateful she didn't follow that up with, "Why didn't you ever tell me?" I've heard other people respond that way, which only puts the responsibility back onto the other person. Children, especially, do not have the responsibility to explain they are being mistreated; the adult is the one who should know and initiate change. Unfortunately, addicted adults often are not capable of acting responsibly, but that does not transfer the burden of responsibility back onto the child.

What Tracy did say was, "I had no idea." A person in the throes of addiction so often has "no idea" of the full effects of that addiction on others, because it creates a self-centered focus. Compounding that tunnel vision is reticence on the part of others, like Kelsey and Kaitlyn, to expose the true nature of their pain, for fear of jeopardizing a relationship already damaged by the addiction. Those girls understood that in any battle with their mother growing up they were going to emerge the losers, so they lived their childhoods surrendered to her rage and persistent negativity. Paradoxically, this surrender to Tracy's anger only suppressed and fueled Kelsey's and Kaitlyn's own anger. Fear and anger became major components of their collateral damage.

Loneliness, fear, and anger are all collateral damage I've seen from addiction. I've also seen the collateral damage of worthlessness, especially when the addiction affects the parent-child relationship. This sense of worthlessness, of being damaged or unlovable, can happen when a child's relationship with a parent is undermined by that parent's addiction. The child does not understand the subtle pressures and complex motivations of the addiction; all they know is they fail to receive that parent's attention or affection. If the child is bold enough to demand that attention or affection, they can run headlong into the strength of the competing addiction; in such cases, the child will lose.

Addiction is a jealous presence, brooking no challenge to its supremacy in a person's life. The voice of the addiction may even speak out against the child, transferring blame and guilt onto them. Children can assume the reason they are not being loved or cared for is because there is something inherently wrong with them. They take on the responsibility for the estrangement within the relationship, and the addiction is not motivated to alter that perception.

Another area of collateral damage from addiction is chaos—the antithesis of peace. The resulting anxiety is a by-product of addiction. The addict anxiously plots out the next encounter with the addiction, fearful and unsure of either the certainty of each occurrence or its ultimate effectiveness. The addict lives a life of uncertainty, which becomes subtly and overtly communicated to others. Those associated with the addict also live with uncertainty, unsure what the next crisis will be and what it will require. Responding to crises can become so engrained in their experiences, especially as children, that life without them can become a foreign experience and seem, inversely, stressful. When crisis is the expected and anticipated norm of childhood, life is robbed of peace. (For an additional resource on this topic, please see my book *Overcoming Anxiety, Worry, and Fear: Practical Ways to Find Peace*.)

Those in relationship with someone struggling with addiction end up struggling themselves, as their lives become entangled with the consequences of that addiction. Perhaps this concept has been best explained through Janet Woititz's groundbreaking 1983 book, *Adult Children of Alcoholics*, which outlines the collateral damage that occurs in children of alcoholics and which she expanded in 1990 to include other dysfunctional family situations. These books are foundational to our recovery work at The Center. An addiction is a devastating cyclone of traumatic events and behaviors that can uproot and unhinge family relationships, causing damage well into the future.

One of the difficult truths of recovery is that it may end the addiction, but it is not guaranteed to undo the damage. The reality of the damage must be accepted and internalized by the recovering addict—a challenging process. The recovering addict, ready to move on, may need to have patience with loved ones whose paths to healing are slower.

Emerging Priorities

We live life surrounded by a sea of choices. The only way to make sense of these competing interests is to filter our choices through priorities. I firmly believe our priorities are determined by what we do rather than what we say. As the adage goes, "Actions speak louder than words." The actions of addiction shout out the priorities of the addicted person. No number of assurances, excuses, rationales, promises, or protestations can drown out an addiction's true priority, which is to continue at any cost.

Those associated with an addict understand, at some level, that they come in below the addiction on a priority list. These loved ones recognize, by the addiction's supremacy, that they have been rejected. This is the reality they've lived with every day of the addiction. They may have cried out in frustration, "If you loved me, you'd stop!" only to watch the addiction continue. They've come to understand the intensity of their love was not sufficient to change the addiction. They can support the change, but they cannot mandate the change. This can leave family members with an overwhelming sense of helplessness. And because this helplessness is painful to experience, they may harbor unresolved anger toward the addicted loved one.

Family members daily live with the harsh reality of the addiction. The addict, however, while actively listening to and believing the voice of the addiction, can fail to see or recognize the damage being done to others. This isn't that surprising; the addict, blinded by the addiction, often fails to see or recognize the damage being done to themselves. Daniel, in the throes of his gambling and drinking, failed to recognize Lisa's increasing isolation and despair. Tracy, blinded by her own anger, failed to recognize Kelsey's and Kaitlyn's increasing estrangement and resentment.

When each was confronted with the truth, they had to readjust their perspectives on the past, the present, and the future. The past could no longer encompass just their pain but had to incorporate the pain their addiction had caused others. Their present had to include relationship reconciliation as part of recovery. Their future had to embrace the difficult possibility that they might experience recovery, including relationship recovery, but their loved one might not.

Are you at a place where you're able to see and recognize the pain your addiction has brought to your relationships? What has your addiction done to your marriage or romantic relationship? Are you a parent? What has your addiction done to your child? What about your parents? How has your addiction changed the relationship you have or had with them? What about other family or friends? What has been your response when confronted by loved ones about your addiction? How many times have you chosen to continue your addiction, regardless of the pain expressed by others? How many relationships have you lost because of your addiction?

Step 8 of the Twelve Steps of Alcoholics Anonymous speaks about the need to make a list of all the people your addiction has harmed. There's a reason this isn't the second or third or even fifth step. Admitting where our direct actions have harmed another human being, especially those we love, is a gut-wrenching personal undertaking. We face tremendous temptation to minimize the negative consequences of our actions, a temptation addiction is all too willing to promote.

My first answer to "Why can't I see what this is doing to others?" is because the addict mind is blinded to the true consequences of the addiction. Whenever you try to see beyond the veil of the addiction, you're presented with all sorts of reasons why you're not really seeing what you're seeing and why others are not really experiencing what they're feeling. Within the haze of addiction, you can't see truth clearly.

My second answer to "Why can't I see what this is doing to others?" is because you don't want to. The truth is too painful, and avoiding pain is an overriding reason for your addiction. You don't want to fully grasp the breadth and scope of the pain your addiction has caused or is causing others, especially those closest to you, those you love, those most vulnerable, those you have a duty to protect. Without the haze of your addiction, you're afraid of seeing the truth clearly; you're afraid of seeing the truth about *you* clearly.

Price Tags

I understand both those reasons. I felt them myself to varying degrees as I struggled to overcome my own addictive behaviors. From those experiences, however, I also know that recovery involves a relentless pursuit of the truth. The alternative—refusing to recognize the truth—carries its own price tag. A price tag that, unfortunately, can also be paid by others.

Frank wasn't there for his daughter, April, growing up. He was always gone, always working, always involved in some activity that was clearly more important than being with her. Sitting down for "tea" with April and her dolls was childish. There wasn't any time for things such as going to the park or taking a walk—that's what April's mother was for. As April got older, Frank never seemed able to attend a curriculum night, a track meet, or a school play. He was too busy doing other things. April remembered her parents fighting over his time away from the family and hearing her father say he was doing it for them. She didn't understand. Nobody had asked her if that's what she wanted. If they had, she would have said no.

Then, in high school, when Frank wasn't traveling as much, he was still gone. He'd close himself off in his office, say he was working, and let it be known he wasn't to be bothered. It wasn't until after April left for college that she found out about her father's prescription drug abuse. She found out only because of his unexpected trip to the emergency room one weekend and her mother's lowered barriers due to exhaustion. April remembered sitting with her mother in the waiting room, shocked at the whispered revelation, and asking how long it had been going on. Her mother's vague response was, "For years."

They took Frank home that night and didn't talk about what happened. He'd seemed surprised and upset that April had gone to the hospital at all. But April couldn't let it go. All this time she'd thought something was wrong with her. She didn't live up to his attention, to his expectations. Was it because she wasn't a boy? Was it because she wasn't smart enough or interested in the right things?

April always wondered why Frank had cut ties with her so early in her life and never seemed interested in gathering them back. She had thought it was her; now, she wasn't so sure. Maybe all this time it was really him. How much time and energy, how many sleepless nights and shed tears had she spent second-guessing herself, distrusting herself, accepting that something else besides her was more worth his time? Recognizing the truth changed everything—how she saw Frank, how she saw her mother, how she saw herself. She knew he'd be furious at her mother for saying something that night. So, she didn't say anything; she'd learned that from him.

Addiction may seek to isolate the addict, but its consequences are anything but isolated. They leach out and contaminate surrounding relationships. Addiction promotes and perpetuates false beliefs, which can affect not only the addicted person but also others. Because of this, addiction has the capacity to transmit itself from person to person to person through the pathway of experienced pain. Truth may be devastating to confront, but from my years of experience, I know that avoiding the truth is worse.

8

Why Is the First Step So Hard?

"Don't say it," Sarah warned.

"Don't say what?" David snapped back at his sister.

"Don't say, 'I know.' Whenever we talk about this, you always say, 'I know,' and you never do anything about it." Sarah was angry at her brother and was not giving him an inch.

What they were talking about was David's addiction and need to go into treatment. I'd been asked to be part of this family intervention, and the start was decidedly rocky, but, then, most of them are.

"I've tried," David insisted.

"No, you haven't," Sarah replied, disgusted. "You've never really tried. You just said what you thought the rest of us wanted to hear and then did what you wanted."

Their parents sat quietly, allowing Sarah to take the lead. She spoke about her pain, reciting a litany of incidents and behaviors that stretched back years. She told David that unless he found a way to stop, they were, all of them, done. At that, both Sarah and David looked over at their parents.

"Tell him!" Sarah insisted to her parents. "Tell him this has to stop!" She was openly crying now. I wasn't sure their parents, especially their father, would be able to go through with it. I could tell she wasn't either. The silence began to drag out as neither parent wanted to speak first.

Leaning in toward them, Sarah pleaded, "Someone has to love David enough to tell him the truth!"

Confronting the Gorilla

The first step in recovery is hard because the truth of the addiction is hard. It's an 800-pound gorilla in the room. The addiction is so powerful and dominating, it sets the agenda.

David's parents had enabled the addiction since he had been a senior in high school, when the future they'd so carefully crafted for their firstborn had, tragically, fallen apart. Since then they'd excused and rationalized; they'd prayed and pretended that the way David was now was an aberration and surely if they just loved him enough, his life would somehow revert to "normal." The truth none of them, except Sarah, had wanted to acknowledge was that David's addiction had become his "normal" well into his twenties.

As I was gauging if this was the time for me to talk, to move the process forward, his mother spoke up. "I won't watch you do this to yourself anymore," she told David. "I love you and it's killing me." Oddly, she had no tears. I could only assume she'd used them up.

With Sarah and their mother united, I watched as David went to the one person his addiction had always been able to rely on with a single plea of, "Dad . . ." Each of us waited to hear his response.

Without looking up, his father said softly, "Don't ask me to help you kill yourself." With those words, David's father finally acknowledged and aligned himself against the gorilla.

I'm not sure where the phrase "800-pound gorilla" came from, but per Merriam-Webster, the first use was in 1976, and it means "one that is dominating or uncontrollable because of great size or power."[1] Interestingly enough, according to the World Animal Foundation, the average size of the largest of the great apes, the mountain gorilla, isn't eight hundred pounds; it's four to five hundred pounds.[2] To me, that makes using this gorilla analogy for addiction even more appropriate, because addiction always puffs itself up to present itself as bigger than it is. This isn't to say that calling out the gorilla of addiction, of whatever size, is going to be easy—because it's not. Addiction will insist change is impossible. Change is possible, but it's also excruciatingly difficult.

People can resist taking that first step, confronting the gorilla, out of fear. To take a step, a person must change position, leave where they are, and move somewhere else. An addiction is a known position; somewhere else can be a frightening and unknown destination. The addict is confronted with thoughts such as *I know where I am now. If I move, where will I go?* I also think the unspoken thought is *If I move, will I be in more pain?*

Fear of Failure

To admit an addiction is to admit powerlessness, as reflected in step 1 of Alcoholics Anonymous.[3] In our culture, we are taught to be self-sufficient, to assert our power in all kinds of situations. We are taught to be empowered, as a function of competence and maturity, in our personal lives, in business, in relationships. Whatever the difficult circumstances, we strive to become masters of our fates and captains of our souls.[4] Imagine, then, our sense of failure when an addiction becomes both captain and master, making us servant and slave.

In Alcoholics Anonymous's step 1, people admit powerlessness and that addiction has made life "unmanageable."[5] Admitting an addiction can feel like admitting incompetence. Other words for incompetent are *inept, inadequate, substandard, inferior, deficient, lacking,* or *unqualified.* Which of us, truly, wants to claim those descriptors? Incompetence means you don't have or aren't able to show the skills necessary to do something successfully. The opposite of success is failure. Almost universally, a true acknowledgment of addiction is quickly followed by a crushing sense of personal failure, whether initially expressed or not.

At eighty-six pounds, Brianna was clearly anorexic, and it was evident to everyone—except her. Brianna doggedly refused to admit she was powerless over her compulsion to starve herself and that her anorexia had made her life unmanageable. She said the only reason she was considering treatment was so she could provide "proof" that concerns about her were "ridiculous" and unwarranted. She was, she assured me, fine. She was just a small, athletic person, and others in her family had much more of a problem with food.

"I'm perfectly happy with my body the way it is," Brianna asserted.

"I'm not so sure your body is perfectly happy with you," I suggested, presenting some dire medical and nutritional information about her condition. Breaking down her barriers took all the information I could gather, along with multiple hours of persistent persuasion over several weeks. The breakthrough came when Brianna could finally articulate her overwhelming sense of personal failure for not living up to her own expectations. She had taken great pride in being the one person in her family to avoid what she called "genetic obesity." Her identity was supposed to be the thin one, the smart one, the outperformer in the family.

Like others I've worked with, Brianna had assigned herself the savior role within the family. As I learned more about her situation, I could see why. The trajectory of her life had been almost meteoric—established through her academic and athletic accomplishments, especially through middle and high school. That pathway was supposed to continue through college and the scholarship she'd been awarded, a scholarship in jeopardy over the past semester due to Brianna's deteriorating health.

She'd tried, as her perfectionism dictated, to "fix" things on her own. But none of those strategies had worked, as a trip to the emergency room during an away game highlighted. In that emergency room, Brianna's increasingly fragile structure of quick fixes and better tomorrows crashed in on itself. The medical diagnosis of her worsening physical condition became impossible for her family—and the school—to ignore any longer. Brianna's place on the team and her scholarship were put on hold for medical reasons.

Sent home, Brianna saw only failure. For her, success had come so early and so often that she had never trusted it. Instead, she lived in fear that the next day or the next task would show she was really a fake. Brianna's identity had been so forged around her successes, she was terrified one epic fail would wipe out all her accomplishments. On the outside, she presented herself as strong and confident, but on the inside, she was a bundle of anxieties and insecurities.

Suffocating Cloud

A sense of failure creates a suffocating cloud of shame. For some people caught in addiction, shame is the demon they've been running from their entire lives. Since as long as they can remember, they've felt defective, inadequate, all those incompetent words, and have run from being labeled as such. The addiction has served as an escape from shame's relentless pursuit, a substance- or behavior-induced time-out. Under the influence of their addiction is the only time they feel inoculated. Asking them to admit powerlessness and failure is like asking them to stand still and let shame roll over them, reducing their lives and sense of self to rubble.

The addiction props up the veneer of maintaining the status quo. For those who believe they have the capacity to and therefore should be perfect, experiencing shame can seem more personally damaging than the effects of the addiction. Those who see themselves as perfect run from shame and use the addiction to escape.

Others gave up on perfection long ago, utterly convinced of their incompetence. Shame isn't something they believe they can run from because shame is their constant companion. Instead, those who see themselves as damaged dwell in shame and use the addiction for momentary respite and even as intentional punishment.

Fear of Exposure

Chapman University's Wilkinson College of Arts, Humanities, and Social Sciences puts out a survey detailing Americans' fears. In 2016, the highest percentage under the category of personal fears was for public speaking, at more than 25 percent.[6] As a public speaker, I can understand why a quarter of the population considers this activity risky business. Putting yourself out in front of other people leaves you exposed. When you're standing up in front of a crowd, with the lights on you and a microphone in front of your face, there's no place to hide. Exposure is a public speaker's occupational hazard and can be frightening. Hiding can seem a safer alternative than exposure.

Shawn's favorite hiding place was a casino, which didn't have to be one of the big ones. In fact, he'd traded the mega-casinos along the interstate for more out-of-the-way strip-mall locations because there was less chance of seeing someone he knew from outside the casino at those places. At the casino, Shawn didn't have to acknowledge anyone. His only interaction was with the machine in front of him. The machine didn't ask anything of him, except to deposit more money. It didn't converse or argue or, more importantly, judge.

The casino floors were always dark, sometimes with a cloud of smoke obscuring Shawn's line of sight even further. To avoid the inevitable foot traffic, he rarely chose a machine on an aisle. Shawn kept his eyes glued to the screen in front of him to discourage idle chatter from the random neighbor. This was his time, his money, his decisions, and he wanted no one to interfere. If he could just concentrate, just put the distractions out of his mind, then, maybe, he could start winning back some of his losses. If not, he still considered the time worthwhile.

Shawn's wife, Tamara, however, did not. When she finally caught wind of his escalating gambling addiction, she was stunned at the amount of money he had squandered. Tamara was livid at the "waste" and what she considered a complete disregard of his family obligations and responsibilities due to his "selfishness." Fortunately, Tamara agreed to engage in some personal counseling herself before she and Shawn joined as a couple to work through the fallout of his addiction. As I've said before, when someone is feeling newly exposed in recovery, the last thing they may be able to withstand is another person calling out every naked flaw.

None of us likes to be totally exposed. Each of us creates masks that enable us to be around other people. If I'm having a rotten day, the last thing I want to do is spread my misery to those with whom I work. Instead, I find a way to compartmentalize my distress so I can function in my job. Is that wearing a mask? Yes, but some masking makes sense. Who, for example, would want to walk around with a conversation bubble over their head, revealing everything they thought to those around them?

I try not to wear masks around those I love, however. There must be some place where I am genuinely authentic and some people with whom I can be open and honest. Masks become dangerous when a person decides never to take them off for any reason or around anyone. Masks can become hiding places—ways to avoid truth, transparency, and authenticity. Masks, then, can be tailor-made for addictions.

In some ways, we live in a "fine" world. "How are you?" "I'm fine, thank you, and you?" "I'm fine too." We're all supposed to be fine. We all want to be fine, because we think we should be, but we're not. We're in pain, we're distressed, we're overwhelmed, we're addicted, but we don't want anyone to know because admitting any of those things means we've failed the "fine test." If we admit to being not fine, we expose our faults, problems, weaknesses, and struggles.

Have you ever answered someone honestly when they asked you how you were? They expected "Fine," they had allotted you enough time to answer "Fine," and then you went into an explanation of how you weren't fine. Sometimes people aren't prepared to hear you're not fine. Once our not fineness is exposed, we can be fearful of how other people will respond.

Fear of Rejection

Admitting an addiction to yourself can be extraordinarily difficult because of the terrifying possibility of rejection. Admitting that addiction to others can seem like walking over hot coals—a prolonged journey of excruciating pain as you watch their incredulous, agonized, or disgusted reactions. Whether it's pornography or prescription drugs or bingeing and purging or sex or whatever the addiction, having to confess the truth to someone else can feel impossible.

Exposure has a shame aspect to it, but shame isn't the end of the fear. The rest of the fear is that you'll also be abandoned, rejected by those you love because of what you've done and who you've become. *Rejection* is another word for *abandonment*, one of our deepest and earliest fears. At the time when you most need others to rally around you, to support you and give you hope, you fear that disclosing the truth will sabotage any chance of them doing so and you'll be left alone to struggle with your addiction.

Family members living with the consequences of an addiction are not always aware of the pathology of addiction and can consider the addiction a moral failure. Telling an addict to "just stop it" implies the person doesn't have the willpower to change their life. While willpower is certainly a large component of recovery, it alone is not enough to overcome the tidal wave of forces pressuring the addict to continue. Just as the addiction becomes a "family affair," so does recovery, because the heavy lifting involved requires a group of people dedicated to honesty, encouragement, and support.

Sydney's parents had no clue she was abusing prescription drugs until she got picked up for a DUI and was in possession of someone else's benzos. She'd tried to quickly stash the pill bottle between the seats when she saw the lights flashing behind her, but that only made it worse. The police found it easily when they searched the car. Neither tears nor protestations of "That isn't mine!" did any good. Sydney was caught, and her parents were going to know.

What would they say? How mad would they be? How long would she be grounded? Would they take away her car? Would they take away her cell phone? Sydney knew she'd trashed their trust. Would they take away their love?

At the root of the fear of rejection is the question, "Will you still love me?" In some cases, the answer has been no. Because people in a relationship have the free will to reject that relationship, no is an ever-present possibility. However, no happens much less frequently than addiction's apocalyptic prophecies to the contrary.

Loved ones have already borne the brunt of much of the addiction's effects, whether those loved ones are aware of the actual addiction. They can't see the wind, but they feel the wind's effects. The estrangement, the jealousy, the chaos, the altered reality have all damaged the relationships. The underlying reasons may not be clear, but the relationships have already experienced significant erosion, and those loved ones have hung on, although the perch on which the relationships sit may have become precarious. The addiction will argue that telling the truth is sure to cause the remaining relationship foundation to cave in and crumble.

In an odd way, I suppose that's a reasonable assumption, yet it's often not what I've seen happen. Instead, the truth, once it is known and as difficult as it is, acts to shore up the relationship. The loved ones finally can begin to put that truth into context with what they've been experiencing. The question "Why is this happening?" is at least answered. With that answer, loved ones can start to understand the structure of addiction and how it affects relationships. They come to realize they've been dealing not only with someone they love but also with an addict, who will act in specific ways due to the addiction.

At first Sydney's parents, when confronted with the truth because of the arrest, were stunned. But as they spent time reframing the events of the past year as well as the feelings they had been afraid to explore even with each other, things became clearer. They began to understand the source of Sydney's moodiness, outright anger, and puzzling apathy. Her struggles with grades, they realized, had less to do with difficult teachers or harder subjects and more to do with her addiction. The distance in their relationship, which they'd lamented but accepted as a product of emerging adulthood, took on a different look. Had their daughter become a different person over the past year? Yes, but now they knew more of the answers as to why.

Addiction wants to leave loved ones in the dark as long as possible. To keep you from admitting and seeking help, the addiction assures you, "If they know, they'll leave." This is such a cruel torment, especially when you consider that the farther a person goes down the road of addiction, the more likely rejection is to happen. Even loved ones have a breaking point—such as when the toxicity of the addictive relationship crosses over a lethal line and, for personal safety or survival, the loved ones must sever the relationship. Fear of rejection is so powerful because rejection is real.

Fear of Relapse

"What are you afraid of?" I asked.

"I can't do this. It's too hard," Ryan replied, which was becoming somewhat of a mantra.

"You've said that before, but what are you afraid will happen?" I needed Ryan to move off his catchphrase and dig deeper into what was supporting it.

"What if I go through all this and it doesn't work?"

"That's your addiction trying to convince you not to try," I said.

To keep you from taking that first step, an addiction will argue that doing so will lead to relapse, not recovery. From this lofty all-or-nothing position, the addiction threatens dire consequences if you're not able to vanquish it completely the first time; the addiction makes sure you know you'll pay a serious price if you mess up, even once (and you will), so why try.

This all-or-nothing reasoning is a hallmark of addiction. I have heard it countless times in statements such as "I can quit anytime I want to," as if an addiction is like a light switch you can just turn on or off. Of course, that switch can always be flipped tomorrow or the next day or when some event happens—never right now.

The addiction says, "I'll just keep doing it for now because I know I can quit anytime." The anytime that never happens is, nonetheless, always kept in reserve to keep you hooked today. But what happens when "I can quit anytime I want" is proven to be a lie? What happens when anytime becomes today and you're not able to quit? Do you have to admit "I can't quit anytime I want"? Taking the first step, forcing anytime to be today, can be like a test of control—your control over the addiction or the addiction's control over you. You may fear that when you take the first step you might not pass the test. Addiction argues that thinking you can pass the test is much better than knowing you can't, so why not put it off until tomorrow?

Fear of Change

There is a phrase, the origin of which seems open to debate, that goes something along the lines of "Better the devil you know than the devil you don't." The accepted meaning is that it's better to deal with something known, even though it's not good, than risk dealing with something different, which could be worse. This is the essence of pessimistic thinking because it assumes that something different is going to be something worse. Addiction is a prolific pessimist.

"I'll lose my friends."

"I'll lose my job."

"I'll ruin my reputation."

"I'll have to quit school."

"I won't have any fun."

"I won't know what to do with myself."

"This is just the way I am."

"How will I deal with the pain?"

Taking the first step is hard because the first step means change. The addictive assumption is that a different life will be worse because nonaddictive strategies to cope with that different life will be less effective. The addiction sees the future without itself as a desolate landscape, stripped of the well-worn handholds and stepping-stones it has provided to help you navigate a treacherous life. Directionless, you'll be left totally on your own, unsupported. This is, again, the catastrophic don't-you-dare thinking of addiction. The worst is always assumed because assuming the worst keeps you trapped.

Addictive thinking assumes the future is to be feared because change is bad. Addictive thinking may admit that the devil you know is bad, but the devil you don't—change—is worse. Addiction's fear takes who you are with the addiction and catapults you into a changed future, with all its implied negatives. But the future only seems bad because the addiction assumes you can't change. A changed you accomplishes a positive, changed future.

Stepping toward a Changed Future

In the all-or-nothing thinking of addiction, when addicts contemplate making a change, they may set their sights on an impossible fantasy recovery where all is made right with the world. But that distance between the unfolding truth of the addiction and such a utopian recovery can appear impossibly long, with too much distance in the middle. Taking the first step is, then, sure to result in a spectacular fall.

The first step in recovery, however, is rarely so dramatic. I've seen first steps be small admissions, faint cracks in the façade. They can come in moments of hesitation or reflective doubt. In *The Addicted Lawyer*, author Brian Cuban, recounting his decades-long battle with drugs, alcohol, and bulimia, writes, "I could take the smallest of steps and stay in my comfort zone. What I didn't know then was that even the smallest of steps into recovery are OK. In reality, even a small step can be life-changing."[7]

Is stepping toward change a risk? Yes, because change involves the future and the future cannot be guaranteed. Having just said the future cannot be guaranteed, where addictions are concerned, I do believe the future can be predicted. From my more than thirty years working with those who struggle with addictions, I know they neither get better nor remain static; addictions progress and get worse.

There is no "accommodating" or "managing" an addiction so its damage remains within "acceptable" limits. This is the bargaining I've seen people try over and over again with their addictions. They know they are bad but don't want to give them up. They just want their addictions to behave and stay within predetermined boundaries. Addictions cannot be domesticated; they are wild and destructive and will always escape enclosure. They cannot be reasoned or negotiated with; there can be no consensus with an addiction. Given an inch, they will take a mile, and then a mile after that, and a mile after that, until you find your life and choices completely out of room.

Out of Room

David was out of room; he just didn't know it. He knew his sister was a lost cause—Sarah had been against him for more than a year. David thought, though, he still had his parents. He knew what they'd said about not wanting to see him kill himself with his addiction, but they'd come through for him before when he really needed them. Armed with that assumption, he didn't enter treatment after the family intervention. Instead, he stoically listened to the family's conditions if he didn't, which involved no more money, no answering late-night calls to bail him out, no allowing him to sleep on the couch, and no contact with them or the extended family. David had frowned when Sarah, his mother, and, finally, his father had said they couldn't keep him from calling, but they'd agreed not to answer those calls. David was told he could leave a message, but they would not respond. The only message they would respond to was that he had gone into treatment.

David nodded, said he understood, and refused. He accepted their assertion to deny contact, never assuming his parents, at least, would stick to it because of the past. This time, he turned out to be wrong. While we couldn't help him at The Center, we were able to help his parents and his sister understand his denial and find a way to keep their hope, and their love, alive—from a distance.

David had nodded and said he understood, but he didn't. He didn't understand the way his addiction had altered his thought patterns and how his brain and body responded in a multitude of ways. David left thinking he was still in charge of his life and his choices. He left not realizing the one choice he had—to admit his addiction and seek help—was the one choice his addiction resolutely did not want him to make.

I wish I could say David changed his mind. He hasn't so far, and I don't think any of his family members have heard from him in years. They don't even know where he is. As Sarah recently said, "We don't know if he's lying dead in a ditch somewhere." That's the future they must find a way to live with because of David's refusal to take the first step.

9

Why Isn't the First Step Enough?

Healing from addiction is not a single step but a process of multiple steps, mostly forward but some back, to achieve the distance necessary to move from addiction to recovery. Brian Cuban puts it this way: "Recovery and feeling like I've created a whole life are constant works in progress, and that just because I've maintained sobriety doesn't mean I've got everything figured out. In recovery, as in life, there will be steps forward and backward. I've never been very good at the cha-cha, but in recovery, I know that missing a step occasionally is only a brief pause in my journey and not the journey itself."[1]

The journey of recovery requires mental and physical healing, which takes time, patience, and perspective that is gained step by step by step. The process of recovery, then, is in opposition to the way addiction operates, which is to promise immediate, in-the-moment, don't-think-just-act relief. The relief of recovery is a slow burn, a fire that must be tended and maintained continuously, lest it dwindle and extinguish. Addiction is anything but patient; recovery must be. Is it any wonder that a straight path to recovery is the anomaly and the cha-cha the norm?

Saying Goodbye

There comes a point when the person decides they are "done" with the addiction. The collective weight of its destructiveness has finally tipped the scales from net-positive to net-negative. The person recognizes they can't continue as they have been. The excuses, the bargaining, the attempts to manage, and the exchanges for other types of addictions have all failed. The one alternative that hasn't been tried—to stop—is the last resort. Sometimes this comes about due to a catastrophic emotional or physical event. For one man, it was when he was high on weed and wrecked his car with his eighteen-month-old strapped inside. For one woman, it was when she woke up in the emergency room when she easily could have ended up in the morgue.

The person sees the horror of their addiction for what it is, and this event cuts through the fog and provides unadulterated clarity. In that moment, fear of continuing within the addiction overwhelms fear of continuing without. In such a ground-shaking revelation, the person finally feels the motivation, drive, and courage to say "No more."

Every addict I've ever worked with has had these moments, which are significant even though they can be highly transitory at first. The addict may have said "No more" because of a particularly nasty consequence, but the goal was to say "No more" to the consequence, not to the addiction. In these cases, they never considered that the addiction would end. As soon as the effects of the consequence dwindled, the addiction was back in full force and was often worse.

Opportunity Cost

A nasty consequence is an "opportunity cost" of addiction; such consequences will continue to happen and intensify, producing gut-dropping repercussions that can shake an addict to their core. Experiencing such defining moments can be essential to recovery, due to the paradigm shift it creates in the addict's mind. Each time, the person's mind is opened to the truth of the addiction; upon recognizing that truth, the person achieves clarity and makes commitments. These commitments to stop and go a different direction are real, albeit short-lived. However, the collective weight of each one puts pressure on the addiction and fortifies the addict's eventual decision to do whatever it takes to stop.

Addiction is prepared to surrender a battle here or there but not the war. When the crisis has passed, the addiction starts to reassert itself. Successful reassertion of the addiction may take hours, days, weeks, or even years. Returning to the addiction is called relapse.

The Reality of Relapse

"Why didn't you tell me it would be so hard?" His surly accusation was loud and clear: I was at fault.

"I don't remember indicating it would be easy," I countered. I did distinctly remember my dilemma just a few short weeks earlier when Kyle had pledged to stop. He'd been almost euphoric as he made his pronouncement, dreaming of how his life would change. I tried, as delicately as I could, to support all his reasons to stop while still being realistic about the potential for relapse. Even mentioning the word had produced an incredulous and defensive response, as if I were calling Kyle's commitment into question and him a liar. Firmly enmeshed in his vision of a life free from addiction, he did not want to hear that his dream would need to be lived out in the real world, day by day, one step at a time. At the time, he'd been soaring above and beyond his addiction; he wasn't interested in my attempts to bring him back to earth. When Kyle crashed, he was furious I hadn't warned him adequately.

Chronic, Not Acute

I've noted that some people consider addiction to be a moral failing. For those with this mind-set, once the moral "compass" is realigned, the addiction will be "cured." This concept of moral failure plays right into addiction's hand by adding to the shame, guilt, and worthlessness that so often encourage the addiction. In the moral failure scenario, you are considered (or consider yourself) weak for becoming overwhelmed by an addiction. To erase the stain of the failure, all that is required (by others or yourself) is to "just say no" and prove you have the moral fiber, the strength to quit. In the moral failure mind-set, relapse is considered continued evidence of weakness, of not trying hard enough. A relapse is unacceptable and unthinkable because it taints and devalues the recovery effort.

Starting in the late 1990s, I watched this moral failure view of recovery and relapse begin to shift as biological and neurological science brought increased understanding to the study of addiction. In 2000, a research study published in the *Journal of the American Medical Association* (*JAMA*) put forth the following proposition:

40% to 60% of patients treated for alcohol or other drug dependence return to active substance use within a year following treatment discharge. One implication is that these disappointing results confirm the suspicion that drug dependence is not a medical illness and thus is not significantly affected by health care interventions. Another possibility is that current treatment strategies and outcome expectations view drug dependence as a curable, acute condition. If drug dependence is more like a chronic illness, the appropriate standards for treatment and outcome expectations would be found among other chronic illnesses.[2]

This study highlighted the idea that addiction—drug dependence specifically—might be better treated as less of an acute, cure-it-now condition and more of a chronic, longer-term condition. As a chronic as opposed to an acute addiction, addiction could then be addressed on an ongoing basis. As in the case of other chronic illnesses, addiction could be understood in terms of an ebb and flow of the condition.

One consequence of viewing addiction within this longer-term framework is that it allows for a corresponding change in the view of relapse. As a longer-term condition, addiction would harbor a greater potential for relapse. The longer the recovery journey, the more steps would be needed and the greater the chance one or more would be backward. Instead of seeing relapse as proof of weakness, relapse could be considered a natural function of the disease progression and, thus, factored in as part of recovery.

As researchers began to consider similarities between addictions and chronic health conditions, they asked themselves how addiction relapse rates compare to chronic health condition relapse rates. The National Institute on Drug Abuse, using information from *JAMA*, compared relapse rates for people with type 1 diabetes, hypertension, and asthma—all considered chronic health conditions—with relapse rates for people with drug addiction.

When I read this, I had to ask myself what relapse would look like for someone with type 1 diabetes or hypertension or asthma. Each of these conditions is chronic but can be managed by adhering to certain pharmaceutical and lifestyle regimens. A type 1 diabetic must adhere to continual blood sugar monitoring and nutritional restrictions as well as pay special attention to physical symptoms. I can imagine such regimens sometimes become overwhelming, leading to anxiety and depression. For some, times of rebellion, when they reject those regimens, may cause their diabetes (or their hypertension or asthma) to become uncontrolled in a type of relapse.

Researchers reported drug addiction relapse rates at 40 to 60 percent, type 1 diabetes relapse rates at 30 to 50 percent, and both hypertension and asthma relapse rates at 50 to 70 percent, concluding, "Relapse is common and similar across these illnesses (as is adherence/non-adherence to medication). Thus, drug addiction should be treated like any other chronic illness; relapse serves as a trigger for renewed intervention."[3] I really like that last conclusion. Relapse serves not as an opportunity for moral indignation but "as a trigger for renewed intervention." This conclusion moves relapse from a brand of weakness and shame to a useful tool in the arsenal of recovery.

In the past, addiction was barred from inclusion in the age-old admonition, "If at first you don't succeed, try, try again." When addiction was considered a moral failure, perseverance, fortitude, and tenacity got divorced from a relapse model of recovery. I have known good, decent, moral people overcome by addiction. They had a burning desire to stop but needed help, support, and treatment to claim recovery, including navigating a recovery road marked by relapse. Each relapse taught them something about themselves, their addiction, and their renewed commitment to try, try again until they achieved success.

Isolation Is a Stone's Throw from Denial

On the surface, Kelli was finding success in recovery; at least I could report to her parents she was showing up for appointments and had clean urinalyses (UAs). I knew Kelli was motivated, as her parents had multiple strings attached to her recovery, such as the return of her car, renewed privileges, and monetary college assistance. With all of that, however, I still had an uneasy feeling about her sobriety. Kelli, resolutely, refused to admit to any fears of relapse and glossed over the temptation to return to alcohol to cope with the stresses of her senior year in high school. Having gone to church all her life, she had her "Sunday school" answers to my questions down pat.

Two weeks from graduation, Kelli relapsed when a weekend barbeque at a friend's house offered more than burgers and chicken. Unbeknownst to the hosting parents, who were blithely manning the grill and serving up chips and potato salad, some of the kids had snuck in alcohol. When the parents escaped to the basement to give the kids "some room," Kelli enhanced her glass of Coke, sure she'd been sober long enough to handle just one drink. Besides, this was a Sunday, and she knew our appointment and the possible UA weren't until Thursday. Kelli's one drink turned into several, and she ended up on her hands and knees, retching up vodka and chips. The house parents called her parents.

During the months we had been meeting weekly, Kelli had put on her "good girl" mask. She had kept herself busy with the final activities of graduation to buffer growing fears of failure. Later, she told me she had been terrified she wouldn't be able to keep up that thin veneer but thought talking about her fears would give them strength. She thought denying them would rob them of power, when in reality it did just the opposite.

Talking openly to others who understand your fears of failure is a core component of recovery. The hiding, secrecy, and isolation of addiction do not automatically end when you put down that drink or those pills or stop that behavior. The masks you've been wearing still fit and seem comfortable. Being open, honest, and transparent can feel unnatural and uncomfortable. Finding a recovery community of people who understand what you're going through firsthand is vital, as others may not understand or empathize with your struggles.

I'm not sure who was more uncomfortable with my suggestion that she attend AA at just barely eighteen—Kelli or her parents. A group met not far from my office in a well-lit, safe part of town. Kelli's reaction to the AA suggestion was that I must be nuts. She'd had a problem, sure, but she was too young to be an alcoholic, too young to go to a group with a bunch of drunks. Her parents' first reactions were similar—why should their daughter go to a group with a bunch of drunks, and besides, someone might recognize her.

None of them wanted to admit Kelli's addiction; they were dealing with it quietly, privately. I wanted Kelli to expand her experience into the recovery community, having seen the value over the years of group synergy. I also knew some members of that group and thought she might be surprised by who attended. They all finally agreed, with the caveat that one of her parents would drive her to the meeting, stay parked outside until it was done, and then drive her home. At the time, she was one of the youngest people attending that AA meeting, but what she lacked in peer support she received in support from those with lots of experience. In more recent years, I've seen additional resources to help young people in recovery, including teenage integration into AA.[4]

The more a person stays isolated in their recovery, the greater the temptation to relapse. Recovery works best with an expanded group of people who provide accountability and camaraderie. When Kelli kept her "recovery community" isolated to only herself and her parents, those were the same people she'd been deceiving while in her addiction. I've found it's much harder to deceive those who have "been there, done that."

Back-Pocket Thinking

While Kelli was terrified of relapsing and tried to hide it, Rob was keeping the possibility of relapse in his back pocket as an option—just in case. He was fine with going through the motions of recovery, learning what he could and gaining back control of his life. He considered these good things. At the same time, Rob didn't consider smoking pot a bad thing. The bad thing was that his pot smoking had gotten out of hand and caused him all sorts of trouble. He was open to finding other coping strategies, but he never really crossed pot off his list; he just kept moving it farther down.

Then the company Rob worked for got bought out by a conglomerate and his middle-management position evaporated. His stress level shot through the roof. His severance package was a joke, and before long, Rob was out pounding the digital pavement looking for another job. Unemployment helped, but he and his wife had just taken on a bigger mortgage. Their oldest child had also gotten braces, and significant COBRA premiums were required to maintain medical and dental coverage. If ever there was a reason to fall off the wagon, this was it. His wife and kids didn't deserve to deal with him the way he was. Nothing he'd tried, no strategy he'd learned, had proved as effective in taking off the rough edges of his anxiety as pot. Besides, Rob assured himself he'd get back into recovery as soon as the "crisis" was over.

An addiction doesn't fit very well into your back pocket. If you think you can keep it there, just in case, you are mistaken. Relapse becomes a greater possibility when you believe you have gained the skills necessary to control the addiction. The operative word is *use*. If you're holding addiction in your back pocket to use "just in case," that addiction won't stay there.

Comparison Shopping

Working with Lauren was a challenge. I knew from our dietitians that she had objected to most of the suggestions they had provided about alternative foods, flavorings, and seasonings. Lauren had usually offered a reason why whatever they had suggested wouldn't work, but she had committed to "try." When she met with me, she told me she felt terrible. Eating healthy wasn't all it was cracked up to be. She was tired of the "rabbit food," the "cardboard" options. In the past, eating had been a real delight; now it was something to be endured.

Lauren wasn't remembering the past correctly. Her eating had been anything but delightful. I reminded her of the bingeing, the gastric distress, the constant preoccupation with food. She countered by saying she still had gastric distress and was constantly preoccupied with food, but now it was with the food she wasn't "allowed" to eat.

Like many others, Lauren entered treatment after years of unhealthy behaviors—for her, it had been two decades. Undoing those patterns and the physical and emotional habits because of them was not going to happen overnight. In the meantime, she was left feeling discomfort. Introducing whole foods into her diet required her gastric system to work harder than it had in years. Refraining from refined and added sugars seemed like punishment. Lauren said she was being cut off from the way she'd rewarded herself in the past. None of it felt good—and neither did she.

Lauren's commitment to recover from her patterns of disordered eating was in danger of collapsing. She was in that precarious position where recovery becomes uncomfortable and challenging. The alternative coping strategies were new and fragile; they appeared ineffective. In addition, gaining some distance from the addiction had caused her past to appear better than it had been.

I've seen those recovering from drugs or alcohol reach this same position. They don't always feel good; sometimes they feel lousy. Because their brain chemistry has been artificially stimulated by these substances, their bodies require time to readjust to the natural production of neurotransmitters, such as serotonin and dopamine, that allow for emotional regulation and a sense of well-being. Recovery hurts, and in contrast, the feel-good promises of the addiction can take on a nostalgic, rose-colored hue.

Physical recovery takes time. Time is required to rebalance your physical systems so you can start feeling good again—naturally.

Time is required to fully integrate nutritional strategies for wellness, instead of pharmaceutical or chemically induced quick fixes. Your body needs time to retrain itself to operate the way it was designed, without interference from outside substances or adrenaline- and cortisol-spiking behaviors. If you expect too much too quick, you'll be tempted to listen to the lie that recovery isn't working, which can lead to relapse.

Stress Relief

Carlos had given up the pills but not the reasons for them. His life was still teetering on the edge of chaos, only now he was more aware of it. Emotionally, Carlos's wife compared him to a prickly pear cactus. Simply put, he bristled. He rarely sat down and relaxed, as if he were making up for time lost to his addiction. His daughter told me she wouldn't mind the "old dad" back for a day, just to have some relief from his constant irritation. Without the pills to "take the edge off," as he once put it, Carlos routinely got into arguments with family members. During a family session in which these issues came up, he angrily remarked that they'd been the ones who'd wanted him to get off the pills in the first place and if they didn't like the way that turned out, it wasn't his fault.

"You've got to work on ways to deal with your stress," I told him.

"I had a way," Carlos tersely responded.

"That wasn't a way," I reminded him. "That was a lie. You weren't dealing with your stress; you were burying it, and it was killing you."

Addiction is powerful for specific physical reasons. It's also powerful for specific emotional reasons. It numbs pain. Carlos was stressed because he was fully experiencing the psychic pain in his life. This pain—from regret, shame, and guilt—was coming out in anger, irritation, and frustration. Instead of owning his own discomfort, he projected it onto others and put the blame on them because they had "demanded" he quit. Lashing out and blaming others are red flags for relapse.

Quid Pro Quo

Recovery wasn't working out the way Linda had thought it would. The deal was she was going to go into treatment, and in exchange, she was supposed to be taken care of after she was discharged. She thought saying no to the addiction would get her a yes from one of her children to let her move in. Of course, none of this was ever articulated to them at the intervention or the family sessions during treatment.

This "arrangement" had been Linda's little secret and the reason she had hung on during recovery. Now as the intensive phase of her treatment was nearing completion, she was devastated to find out none of her children wanted to share their homes with her. They expected her to continue to live on her own. Linda felt betrayed.

Linda's addictive behavior was relationship dependency. Her obsessive neediness and smothering behaviors had alienated her husband years earlier, causing emotional, if not physical, estrangement before his death. Once he passed, her addiction transferred full force onto her adult children. The incessant demands, histrionics, and crises were tearing apart those bonds as well. Linda's children loved her, but as her son admitted, he wasn't sure he liked her—at least the way she was. Her children wanted relationship but also desperately needed boundaries.

Sometimes recovery can become entangled in a quid pro quo situation. The "bargain" may be overt, sometimes implied. In Linda's case, the bargain was one-sided. In a quid pro quo situation, there is an assumption that those who are asking you to give up the addiction are supposed to give up something in return. In her case, in exchange for giving up her addictive behavior, Linda expected her children to fill whatever needs had been provided by the addiction. Unequal, implied bargains are unstable and provide a greater chance of failure and eventual relapse.

Are We There Yet?

Do you remember being a kid on a long road trip? Maybe it was to visit relatives in another state. When you first got into the car, you were excited about where you were going and how much fun you'd have. You weren't paying attention to what it would take to get there. At some point along the drive, when the excitement had worn off and fatigue and boredom had set in, you plaintively called out in despair, "Are we there yet?" I've heard a version of this childhood sentiment come out of the mouths of just about every addict I've worked with.

When you keep taking step after step after step, sometimes you get tired of walking. The journey of recovery is a long one, and there will come times when you are fatigued and disappointed, doubtful of ever reaching your destination. You're tired of constantly fighting against the urges to continue in the behavior. You want the trip to be over. You just want to be "cured."

Addiction doesn't work that way, which is why it is better viewed as a chronic condition instead of an acute one. I believe we, as a community, must view addiction this way to provide people with the support they need to be successful in recovery— recovery that will include the high potential for relapse. As one study concluded, "Ultimately, individuals who are struggling with behavior change often find that making the initial change is not as difficult as maintaining behavior changes over time. . . . It is imperative that policy makers support adoption of treatments that incorporate a continuing care approach, such that addictions treatment is considered from a chronic (rather than acute) care perspective."[5]

Relapse is prevalent because addiction is persistent. It has the power to blindside those who do not maintain a sense of vigilance—and even those who do. The power of addiction is a reason why many in the recovery community stress the need to "work the program." Working the program means maintaining accountability through individual mentoring and group participation. When recovery is kept as a present focus, addiction from the past has less opportunity to infiltrate. Knowing you can fall helps motivate and encourage you to watch your step in the present.

Note that I said in the present and didn't include the future. Recovery, I've come to understand, is best viewed in the here and now. When people in recovery speak about the reality of focusing on today, they talk about "one day at a time." The "Are we there yet?" question is a future-focused question. It ties your happiness to some future event, implying that "here" is unsatisfactory and only being "there" will change that condition. Now is the only time, and here is the only place—that's guaranteed. What happens then and there cannot fully be known. As Jesus said in the Sermon on the Mount, "Therefore do not worry about tomorrow, for tomorrow will worry about itself. Each day has enough trouble of its own."[6]

Recovery for the rest of your life can be a daunting challenge, especially when you have a bad day. Committing to recovery today, one day at a time, puts the challenge into a more confined package for you to carry. Don't worry about tomorrow, Jesus said; take charge of today and let tomorrow worry about itself.

Recovery happens when you commit to making here the place you want to be. Recovery happens when you stop looking anxiously out the window of your life for some better place and begin enjoying and appreciating where you are now. When joy and appreciation infuse your life, addiction has a reduced chance of regaining a foothold.

Riding the Wave

While physical cravings can often diminish over time, I have been surprised by the resiliency of psychological urgings. The physical self may have adjusted to life without the addiction, but the emotional self can feel the pull of the addiction much longer. Urgings and cravings are unwanted physical and psychological companions along the recovery journey. Strategies for dealing with urgings and cravings, therefore, need to be incorporated into recovery coping skills.

At The Center, we utilize a type of therapy called Dialectical Behavior Therapy (DBT), created by Dr. Marsha Linehan, who is a professor at the University of Washington. We have found the skills taught as part of DBT to be extremely well received and helpful to those we serve with a wide variety of mental health, substance use, and medical issues. One tenet of DBT is a concept called "mindfulness," which is the practice of being aware of what you're thinking, feeling, and doing. Mindfulness also includes being aware of what you feel urged to do.

One study I read sought to understand how the practice of mindfulness could be utilized as part of relapse prevention. Speaking about mindfulness, the study concluded: "From this standpoint, urges/cravings are labeled as transient events that need not be acted upon reflexively. This approach is exemplified by the 'urge surfing' technique, whereby clients are taught to view urges as analogous to an ocean wave that rises, crests, and diminishes. Rather than being overwhelmed by the wave, the goal is to 'surf' its crest, attending to thoughts and sensations as the urge peaks and subsides."[7] Urges will happen. Recovery, then, is not leaving the water; recovery is learning to successfully ride the wave.

I Got This

I know people who have been sober for decades and still identify themselves as alcoholics. For some, this may seem like a defeatist attitude. On the contrary, I consider it a prudent attitude, because I have seen the power of addiction strike back at people after decades of dormancy. Relapse is possible when you think you've left the water, only to get pulled under by a powerful wave. Relapse is possible when you think your addiction was an acute "cured" event instead of an ongoing chronic condition that must be monitored.

Relapses tend to occur when people believe they have been "cured" and can return to substances, behaviors, or attitudes from the past without consequence. After a few days or weeks of sobriety or refraining from a behavior, they say to themselves, "I got this," only to have the addiction say, "Gotcha." Addiction is complex, affecting the whole person and creating a tangled web of emotional, relational, intellectual, physical, and spiritual threads that require time and patience to unravel.

Allowing for time and having patience are attributes that I'm not sure are being supported by our current state of society. We are increasingly impatient, as we are conditioned by technology toward instant results. Our concept of time is being altered by that technology, with "slow" and "fast" taking on new definitions. In some ways, recovery should stay "old school," with the understanding of how time, patience, and face-to-face accountability lead to success. In other ways, recovery needs to become even more "new school" and shed the stigma of moral failure.

Whenever a relapse happens, you must decide what to learn from the relapse. Addiction wants you to conclude you are worthless, that you'll never be able to change because change is too hard and you're not worth good things in your life. Recovery wants you to accept responsibility, learn from what happened, and determine how to gain support to continue your recovery. Addiction wants you to return to isolation. Recovery wants you to reach out to others. Addiction is the voice of defeat. Recovery is the voice of hope. On any given day, only you can decide which to follow.

10

How Can I Put My Life Back Together?

"I've made so many mistakes. I screwed up so many things." Despair was evident in Jacob's voice and written across his face. "How can I put my life back together?"

People with addictions keenly notice voids in their lives and have a compulsion to "fix" what they perceive is wrong. Often they felt damaged prior to the addiction, and that damage is part of what fueled their descent into addiction in the first place.

The Need to Fix

Addiction masquerades as a great fixer. You tell yourself it helps make you feel better—makes you more confident, allows you to forget the pain, and lets you be a different person. It promises to fix, but it does the opposite. Instead of alleviating the need to fix, addiction contributes to the damage, increasing an already desperate desire to fix.

Once a decision is made to stop the addiction, the need to fix doesn't necessarily go away. In some ways, once the fog of addiction lifts, the person more clearly sees a devastated personal landscape and feels more damaged than ever. They are left alone, without the crutch of the addiction, to endure the compulsion to fix. The task of fixing, of putting life back together, can appear overwhelmingly difficult, which garners immediate and forceful agreement from the addiction.

Depending on your personality, you may have different ways of approaching the task of fixing what is broken. Are you a person who, upon breaking something, immediately rushes to repair it as quickly as possible? Paper it over, cover it up, slap some paint on it and call it good? To you, being broken is unsafe and vulnerable; you need a solution as soon as possible.

Or are you a person who is paralyzed when something breaks? You are left staring at the brokenness without an idea of what to do. To you, being broken is unsafe and vulnerable; you look to others to fix it for you.

The Land of Broken Things

Maria grew up covering over her mother's "problems." Those were private, and it was her job to clean up after her mother—sometimes literally and sometimes figuratively—creating plausible rationales for younger siblings and outsiders. Creatively covering when things went wrong was a learned skill, and Maria admitted to getting very good at it. When something "broke," her job was to move, mobilize into fix-it mode, sweep it up, and pretend it was never broken in the first place. As an adult, Maria took that skill and earnestly applied it to her own brokenness.

Tim grew up in a household in which other people solved his problems. He was blamed for them, often vehemently, but never allowed to make good himself. Tim's father considered him incompetent. After all, Tim had caused the problem in the first place, so why would he be trusted to fix it? Tim's job was to stay out of the way, endure the tongue-lashing, and watch how competent people cleaned up his messes.

Brokenness most often prompts different responses from people, I've found, based on how they were raised. Dealing with brokenness happens early in childhood, and the family structure dictates how brokenness—and fixing—is handled. Children learn what happens when something breaks, how blame is handled, how shame is handled, and lessons about forgiveness—whether extended or not. Brokenness informs a child that things are not always right in the world, that whole things can become broken. These are foundational lessons with lasting impressions that affect how a person deals with their own brokenness as well as that of others. I don't find it strange, then, that one of the enduring poems in childhood literature deals with the subject of brokenness.

Humpty Dumpty

Remember Humpty Dumpty? He sat on a wall, had a big fall, and none of the king's horses or men could put him back together. End of story but no happily ever after—just brokenness. This simple, four-line lyric teaches children several lessons. One is that falls can cause brokenness. Another is that broken things are hard to put back together. Still another is that success, even with effort, is not a given. And, finally, not everyone called in to help can. Such adult themes clothed in a children's nursery rhyme.

The lessons of Humpty Dumpty apply to addiction, because addiction breaks things and those broken things need fixing. Pretending that isn't true may be tempting, but it is a lie. After the perpetual and painful lies of an addiction, the last thing anyone—whether family members, friends, or the addicts

139

themselves—needs to deal with is more lies. Those experiencing addiction must be prepared to live in a world, and with relationships, where Humpty Dumpty is broken and may not get put back together again.

I always wondered what happened to Humpty Dumpty after he couldn't be put back together. Did he just lie at the base of the wall in pieces? Did he get partway put back together, maybe with little bits of him trailing behind him? Was he put together enough to go off with the king's horses and men? I'm an optimist, so I tend to choose the latter.

What about you? Are you the sort of person who, upon receiving a gift that chips or cracks or has any sort of imperfection, considers that gift now trash? Are you the sort of person who places things on high, unattainable shelves to keep them pristine? Do you remember fondly every scrape and bump, ding and dent to chronicle the life and joy of an object? Or do you look at that same well-worn object as less than it was? Do you appreciate store-bought things over homemade? Do you say thank you for the lumpy, off-kilter gift without having any intention of proudly displaying it? Depending on how you answered those questions, your world may be one where there is no place for Humpty Dumpty. I cannot emphasize enough that to understand lessons from the Humpty Dumpty world we live in, you first must accept a world where things (and people) are allowed to be broken.

Humpty-Dumpty Lessons

- *Falls can cause brokenness.*

    One of the joys I remember when my kids were babies was throwing them up in the air and letting them experience free fall. I knew I was going to catch them, but when they were very little, they didn't know they needed to be caught. They hadn't yet learned that falls can cause brokenness. Once they got older, they figured that out but also knew I would catch them, so they still enjoyed the game.

Broken people can be deceived by addiction, which appears to play the same game—it promises to catch them when they fall but doesn't. Addiction encourages them to climb to the top of a steep wall and then pushes them off, without having any intention of catching them. After broken people gather what pieces they can at the bottom, addiction entices them to climb up and do it again, creating more brokenness with every fall. Addiction is a liar that teaches broken people to both tell and believe lies. In recovery, the addicted person must come to terms with both types of lies—the lies they have told others and the lies they have believed. Those who wish to support a broken person must come to recognize the lies they've been told as well as realize the depths of the lies the addicted person has told themselves.

• *Broken things are hard to put back together.*

I seem to constantly run up against a frustrating truth— things take longer than I expect. This is especially true when trying to fix something that's broken. I can see so clearly what is wrong and have it straight in my mind what needs to happen to fix it, but the amount of time I assign as reasonable for the task is, chronically, less than needed. I think the fix is taking too long, only because I've underestimated the reasonable repair time.

Broken things can be difficult to get my hands around. They slip because the handholds that are supposed to be there aren't anymore. There can be jagged parts that must be watched out for or I'll wind up with a puncture, scrape, or cut. When that happens, I'm tempted to blame the broken thing for being broken instead of myself for not being more attentive.

141

I can't always find the original piece to repair what is broken. Sometimes I'm left to use something that isn't great but works as well as possible. Because the shape isn't exact, my repair can look lopsided. Even though it works, I can be left feeling unsatisfied with the repair.

Broken people are like broken things, and the addicted person and those in relationship with them must accept the truth about broken things—they take longer to fix than you think. They can be difficult to get your hands around, and sometimes you can get hurt trying to repair them. Even after they're fixed, they may not look exactly like you want.

- *Success, even with effort, is not a given.*

Humpty Dumpty didn't have some of the king's horses and some of the king's men; he had them all, and together they couldn't put him back together. This was a concerted, coordinated effort, but it wasn't enough. When attempting to fix broken things, we sometimes generate a sense of entitlement. We come to believe we are "owed" success because of how hard we've tried. This doesn't work well with objects. Because I've spent two hours trying to fix my alternator doesn't mean I'm owed a car that starts, even though I think that during my third visit to the auto parts store.

This doesn't work with people either. Because an addicted person is trying doesn't mean success is guaranteed. On the contrary, recovery necessarily includes the reality of relapse for this very reason. The defeatism of addiction would say don't even try. Yet if you don't try to repair broken things, they will certainly remain damaged.

Have you ever tried to fix a broken item, only to have it break immediately after? When that happens to me, I have a choice to make. I can either give up or learn from what happened. By evaluating what went wrong, I can adjust my strategy to ensure my next repair lasts longer. This, I believe, is the essence of the recovery process—learning how to make repairs last longer.

- *Not everyone called in to help can.*

  It's always seemed odd to me that horses were called in to try to help Humpty Dumpty. Horses tend to trample things on the ground, not put them back together. Sometimes the reason broken things don't get fixed is because the ones asked to help aren't able to do so. I've seen this happen in some intervention situations. What is needed is compassionate, intentional intervention. Yet family members become overwhelmed or present as angry or shaming, overflowing with bitterness or frustration. They may even exude exhausted apathy. The focus of the intervention switches from a desire to help the hurting addicted person to a free-fall venting session for the hurting family. I've found these types of interventions have a low percentage of success.

  Please don't misunderstand me. Each of these family reactions can be entirely valid. Loved ones can be deeply angry and disappointed with the actions of the addicted person. They can experience extreme bitterness and frustration over what has transpired. They can even arrive at a place of emotional numbness and weariness. If a loved one comes from any of these places, they may not have the capacity to assist with the intervention or even the recovery.

  Not everyone affected is able to assist with the repairs. Sometimes a person must concentrate on repairing themselves (whether they realize it or not) and is not available to assist anyone else. Other times a person desires to jump in and help but doesn't have the tools needed to really assist. Groups such as Alcoholics Anonymous and Narcotics Anonymous include sponsors in recovery programs for a reason. Each person brings different tools to the repair called recovery and is available to help at various times.

One Piece at a Time

Jacob despaired, admitting to his many mistakes and asking how he could put his life back together. I'd given him the only answer I had, which was "one piece at a time."

My answer was in line with the AA philosophy of one day at a time, one step at a time. Recovery is very much a journey, and I'm reminded of the adage "The journey of a thousand miles begins with a single step." I've always wondered where that saying came from. According to the BBC, "In this quote, Lao Tzu is trying to express that great things start from humble beginnings. In the original, the text refers to '1,000 li journey.' A li is an old Chinese measure of distance which converts to 360 miles or 576 km."[1] I'm even more impressed now that I know the journey wasn't 1,000 miles but 360,000 miles! Recovery, at the start, can seem like a long, long distance away. But recovery is not the destination; it is the journey, which is taken step by step by step. Or as I indicated to Jacob, piece by piece by piece.

Once you admit you're broken, you must agree to look at reconnecting the pieces of your life that addiction has torn apart. Your relationships may be strained, estranged, or severed. Your health may be compromised. Your finances may be in shambles. Your career may be crumbling. Your faith may be lost. In my experience, most people with an addiction come for help later rather than sooner. The longer they wait, the more fractured their lives become and the more pieces there are to pick up. The more pieces, the longer the process takes.

Relational Pieces

I am not one of those people who enjoys putting together jig-saw puzzles, especially the megapiece variety with an intricate picture. Engaging in this form of "recreation" falls right below root canals on my list of favorite things to do. I have, however, on occasion, participated at family gatherings when these types of puzzles have been set up on a central table with many chairs along the edges. I've found this activity is better when done with others.

Imagine how daunting it is to be broken, realizing you need to put together the pieces of your life with nobody there to help. That is what addiction can do—siphon off support. While addiction is weaving its stranglehold on your life, it is also twisting and breaking connections to others who could provide help and support just when you need them most.

I've been in situations in which family members, when confronted, have met an addict's assertion of "This time, I mean it" with stoic, almost apathetic, disbelief. The door of relationship has been slammed shut, and the addict is not allowed back in, no matter how much they knock. The spoken or unspoken response is "Prove it and don't come back until you do—and maybe not even then." In a Humpty-Dumpty world, some people refuse to engage in difficult puzzles of reconstruction. Whether those reasons are accepted or seen as invalid, the result is the person in recovery must start the process alone.

The first piece that must be put into place is the one that says you are worth being put back together. This isn't a value judgment anyone else can make for you—you must make it for yourself. Depending on the willingness of others in relationship with you, you may find yourself sitting alone at the table with the "1,000 li journey" puzzle in front of you. If you wait for someone else to start the reconstruction, you could be waiting a long time. Instead, you need to see the value in starting the process, regardless of when or if others agree to join you.

The relationship that stands as the foundation for the other relationships in your life is the relationship you have with yourself. This is the relationship that was first and foremost damaged by the addiction. Before you started lying to others, you started lying to yourself. Before others will believe you're telling the truth, you must relentlessly be truthful with yourself. Recovery depends on your capacity to tell and accept the truth—not for a certain outcome or specific reason or to try to convince someone you've changed but because truth is a powerful shield against an addiction's attempts to gain you back.

The healthier the relationship with yourself, the healthier your relationships with others. Not only does truth allow you to see yourself more clearly, but it also allows you to see others more clearly. This capacity to see others more clearly is vital to recovery because the types of people and relationships that often survive within an addiction have been forged from the addiction. Other, healthier relationships can be intentionally jettisoned because they do not support the addiction. Healthier relationships, in active competition with the addiction, can become cut off and wither. The more truthful you live your life going forward, the more you encourage healthier people to take another chance on you.

Emotional Pieces

Addiction numbs pain. As the effect of the addiction begins to wear off, just like an anesthetic, the pain can come roaring back because it was never gone, merely numbed. In some ways, the pain can be worse because the addiction kept you from dealing with its source, allowing it to grow and fester and putrefy. When the wound finally gets opened to the air, it hurts and it stinks.

Recovery allows you to start feeling again. I've watched people sob uncontrollably for a long, long time. Invariably, they will apologize, as if they've done something wrong. And often they are not apologizing for their pain but the expression of their pain. I've seen people be furious, sad, remorseful, incredulous. They have a gamut of emotions they've been desperately trying to contain.

Putting the pieces back together must include finding a new context for the emotions that supported the addiction. Those emotions are there; they exist and pretending they don't is playing back into the hand of the addiction. Instead, they need to be brought forward, understood, and put back into places that support recovery.

As these repressed emotions are released, they allow a healthier flow for day-to-day emotional responses. I've found those in recovery can need help relearning what those healthier channels of emotional release look and feel like. Dealing with sadness without sinking into despair; weathering momentary frustrations without catastrophizing; accepting joy and happiness in the moment without worrying about the future; and tolerating difficult people without isolating or withdrawing are just a few examples. Learning to adjust to these universal rhythms can help establish a new "normal"—one that looks less like the addiction and more like real life.

Intellectual Pieces

A piece of recovery that may take time to fit into place can be intellectual. I was struck by this recently as I was reading the Brian Cuban book I mentioned earlier. Brian talks about how his addiction downgraded his intellectual capacity to perform as an attorney, which makes perfect sense. He also, however, talks about how he never wanted to be an attorney in the first place. Becoming an attorney was what he considered a path of least resistance, which I found impressive, given the intellectual rigors of becoming licensed. While in recovery, he made the decision to stop practicing law. I have worked with others in recovery who have realized they desired a change regarding where they were intellectually or professionally. In recovery, and to further that recovery, people have changed careers, pursued education, or taken up different hobbies and activities.

Addiction wants to keep you stuck, with limited options. One option, really—the addiction. Recovery can reveal possibilities, including intellectual pursuits, because the energy and drive of the addiction can now be channeled down different paths. Recovery can mean discovering new interests or rediscovering interests long buried.

Physical Pieces

Some pieces cannot be put back in the same place. A physical piece of a forty-year-old in recovery is not going to fit back into a twenty-year-old slot. Many things can be recaptured in recovery, but time is not one of them. When putting physical pieces back into place, you must work with the pieces you have, not the pieces you had when you started the addiction, especially if the addiction has been years or decades in the making.

Addictions, behavioral addictions but especially substance addictions, take a physical toll on the body. This may seem like bad news but is actually good news, because once the addiction stops, that damage to the body ceases and the body can start a process of healing. When the addiction was in control, the body was co-opted to serve it. Freed by recovery, the body can return to using its energy to rebuild, replenish, and renew itself and you in the process. Physical healing runs its own course with its own timeline, which may or may not coordinate neatly with the timeline for other pieces of recovery.

At The Center, medical and nutritional professionals partner with mental health and chemical dependency professionals to function in tandem to harness the healing powers of the body, working toward whole-person recovery. Many of those in recovery are unaware of the synergy between their physical and psychological health. When the whole person is factored into recovery, where once the body was an unwitting participant in the addiction, the body can now become an engine of health and renewal to support the other pieces of recovery.

Sometimes those in recovery can be anxious or fearful of the physical consequences of their addiction. They may have avoided going to a physician for years. Facing the truth of these physical consequences can be difficult, especially hearing that certain damage is permanent. Recovery, like repairs, is not universally pristine. Recovery does not return a person to their original state. Part of living in recovery may mean learning how to manage the physical effects of the addiction after the addiction is gone.

For this reason, I believe strongly in creating a professional recovery team that includes medical professionals who understand and are experienced in working with people in recovery. These professionals are alert to the issues with prescribing pain medication to recovering substance addicts and make sure to include behavioral oversight during medical appointments. They understand and appreciate the role of nutritional support for medical and mental health issues and aren't offended by the inclusion of dietitians and alternative medicine providers on the recovery team.

Your health is a finite resource that must be protected and supported, a foundational piece of whole-person recovery. It is often difficult to come to terms with the physical consequences of your addictive behaviors, especially if outside substances were involved, including food. Avoiding the truth, however, is a continuation of addictive thinking. Recovery is about accepting where you are now and finding a way to move forward.

Spiritual Pieces

I'll be dealing with spiritual aspects of healing from addiction in the final chapter, but I wanted to mention it here, because so many questions that arise in recovery are what I consider life questions. And life questions are often deeply spiritual. They deal with purpose and meaning, value and worth, failure and redemption. Having been rendered powerless by an addiction, people can have questions about things more powerful. As they seek to reconstruct their lives and reinforce their recoveries, they can look to find places to put these spiritual pieces.

As a Christian, I work with Christians, but I also work with people of different faiths and no faith. People may phrase these life questions differently, but I've rarely found someone who doesn't ask them on some level. Addiction decimates hope and seeks to supplant faith in anything else. Once the power of the addiction is countered, the natural quest for meaning that finds its expression so often in spirituality is restored and these pieces become relevant again.

Recovery, then, is an intricate tapestry of many parts that mirror the complexity of the human condition. The person who comes to understand their brokenness cries out, "How can I put my life back together?" This question is often asked with shades of despair, but I choose to greet the question with optimism, hope, and joy. I am optimistic because even asking the question means the person desires a return to wholeness. I am hopeful because the question indicates a willingness to reject the lies of addiction and seek after the truth. I am joyful because I've seen what's happened to far too many people who refused to even ask the question.

11

Do I Deserve to Put My Life Back Together?

Angela was having a difficult time. Three years into her recovery, she had just undergone her second relapse. Discouraged and ashamed, she contemplated giving up, close to concluding she was a "lost cause."

"I'm never going to get over this."

"Never," I reminded her, "is a very long time. Why not just try for today?"

"What good is today," Angela asked, "if I can't have tomorrow?"

"Why can't you have tomorrow?"

She thought, frowning and darting her eyes back and forth over the carpet. "I can't have tomorrow," Angela finally answered, "because I don't deserve it."

"Why not?" I asked.

Tears welled up in her eyes, and her voice broke. "I can never go back and make up for what I did, the people I hurt. Why do I deserve to be happy when I've made people I love so miserable?"

Facing Shame

The road to recovery is not easy. Along the way people can find their resolve to heal weakened by feelings of worthlessness and regret. To move forward, they must find ways out of these personal prisons, even when shame, blame, and guilt threaten to block their path.

Shame has been defined as "a painful feeling of humiliation or distress caused by the consciousness of wrong or foolish behavior."[1] I'm not sure true recovery can take place without facing a sense of shame. In addiction, people can commit wrongful acts and participate in foolish behavior without a conscious realization of the damage being done. In recovery, people come face-to-face with the reality of their words, actions, thoughts, and behaviors without the false shielding of the addiction. Their eyes are opened and the picture isn't pretty.

While intoxicated, Terry said and did things he could hardly remember or couldn't remember at all. When others tried to explain the truth about his drinking, Terry brushed them off as lying or exaggerating, even as jealous. He wouldn't admit to being drunk; he remembered being funny, popular, and attractive. In recovery, Terry took off the mask and saw the truth, cringing in shame at hearing some of the stories and seeing some of the pictures he'd routinely dismissed before. He reached a point where he told me, "I really don't want to know any more."

Once you've become conscious of wrong or foolish behavior, you have choices to make in recovery. The pain of shame can cause you to reject that your behavior was wrong or foolish—the minimizing I talked about earlier. You can also maximize the shame, as she did, using it to justify the conclusion that Angela didn't deserve to be happy and healed.

There must be some sort of middle ground, where shame is experienced and integrated into recovery instead of used against it. In our culture, humiliation is considered negatively, meaning "to reduce (someone) to a lower position in one's own eyes or others' eyes: to make (someone) ashamed or embarrassed."[2] However, it wasn't always that way. The origin of the word *humiliate* comes from the mid-sixteenth century and derives from a Latin verb that means "made humble" or "to bring low." I cannot tell you how many times I have heard the expression that a person in active addiction just isn't ready to engage in recovery because they haven't "hit bottom" or gone "low" enough. For many, hitting bottom or being brought low by the addiction is the point where recovery begins.

Recovery, then, could be called an act of becoming humble about the truth of the addiction and about yourself. Being humble or having humility does not seem to carry the same negative connotations as humiliate or humiliation. Humble is defined using words like *unpretentious* or *modest*. In some ways, addiction produces humiliation, but recovery can turn humiliation into humility.

In the bravado of his addiction, Terry tended to think more highly of himself than was true and, consequently, less of others. Once he experienced shame, he found a way to accept his brokenness, becoming sensitive and compassionate not only toward himself but also toward others. By smashing that artificial pedestal he'd built for himself, Terry experienced relief and found community.

Facing Blame

A natural human reaction when confronted with something amiss is to vehemently proclaim, "Don't blame me!" Addiction will use blame in whatever way necessary to produce its desired result of keeping you dependent on it. If you are the sort of person who tries to avoid blame at any cost, addiction will consistently convince you that something or someone or even "the world" in general is responsible for the bad things that happen to you. If you want to avoid blame, addiction will gladly assist by pointing in every direction but inward.

If you are the sort of person who absorbs blame, addiction will agree that you are the source of all things bad. It will consistently remind you of your faults, emphasizing and exaggerating them. These faults will be used as prima facie evidence that you are bad and don't deserve good things, including recovery.

Because blame is so misused in addiction, how to deal with blame honestly and productively becomes one of the hardest questions to answer in recovery. When assigning blame, where is the line between the addiction and the person? In responsibility, where does the addiction end and the person begin? The answers to these questions affect not only the person with the addiction but also those in relationship with that person. As I've talked about, in years past, the line measured heavily on the side of the person being to blame. More currently, the line is shifting to the addiction taking on more of the responsibility, along the lines of a chronic illness.

The only satisfactory answer to the question of assigning blame is that the addicted person must decide where that line falls. This is integral to the recovery process. Taking on blame, or assigning responsibility, is a task that must be reserved for the person, even though others may want to jump in. Only by undertaking this task for himself or herself can the person truly own and accept the outcome.

Like recovery, accepting blame or responsibility can take a series of forward and backward steps. As recovery progresses, the person continues to integrate new understandings and insights about self, about the addiction, and about others. These understandings and insights act as stepping-stones to even greater truth and awareness. Recovery, then, is not unlike the maturation process from childhood, through adolescence, and into adulthood. A person fully in recovery will have greater depth of understanding than a person newly in recovery. When this process is rushed, there is an elevated danger of stumbling or falling. But before you can run, you first must walk.

Simply put, accepting responsibility is not a task that can be accomplished overnight. Those who reject responsibility can require time to shoulder the weight of addiction's consequences. Those who absorb responsibility may need time and support to throw off the suffocating weight of addiction's lies. Recovery is advanced when people accurately assess their responsibility in the addiction by understanding themselves as well as the addictive process.

Assigning blame and accepting responsibility are not bad things. On the contrary, when done properly, they can be empowering. This concept transcends addiction and encompasses recovery from a variety of issues. When you understand what you are responsible for, then you know what you have the power to change. The Serenity Prayer is a beautiful example that illustrates this concept: "God, grant me the serenity to accept the things I cannot change, courage to change the things I can, and wisdom to know the difference."[3] Recovery means you take the blame or accept responsibility for only those things you can change. Recovery is also realizing that there are more things you can change than an addiction would ever admit.

Facing Guilt

Shame has been called feeling bad for *being* wrong, while guilt has been called feeling bad for *doing* wrong. One involves actions, while the other touches essence. Addiction uses actions to condemn essence by saying that, because you are addicted, you are worthless; because you are guilty, you are shameful. During an addiction, you feel guilt about actions you've taken; the weight of that guilt produces shame about who you've become as a person. The addiction uses the interconnection between guilt and shame to keep you dependent and complicate your path to recovery. Therefore, unhooking guilt from shame can be a way to strengthen recovery.

Addiction may have distorted your feelings of guilt, wrapping your essence (your sense of who you are) with your actions (what you did while addicted). Addiction will also try to turn what has been called "proportionate guilt" into "disproportionate guilt." Proportionate guilt would be feeling guilty for something you did or said while addicted. Disproportionate guilt would be feeling guilty for simply being alive and addicted. Proportionate guilt says, "I did bad." Disproportionate guilt says, "I am bad."

If your barometer that measures shame and guilt, proportionate and disproportionate guilt, has been compromised by addiction, how can you recalibrate in recovery? The most effective strategy I've come across is encapsulated in steps 8 through 10 of the twelve-step process. Steps 8 and 9 direct you to make a list of the people you have harmed and accept responsibility by making amends. Making a list means saying, "I'm guilty," to a range of harmful actions, and the attitudes and behaviors fueling those actions. Once you've admitted guilt, you seek to amend those actions where possible. Step 10 says you must continue to track your actions going forward and be ready to promptly admit guilt.[4]

I believe guilt's true purpose is not to condemn a person's essence but rather to protect it. Each of us is guilty of doing what we consider wrong, of violating our personal values or beliefs. When this happens, a sense of guilt reminds us of what we consider important. We hurt because we've injured something personally valuable. An addiction will lie and say that guilt is bad—something to be avoided, numbed on the one hand or crammed down our throats as proof of our worthlessness on the other. In recovery, guilt can be harnessed to help us direct our steps going forward. By understanding and making amends when we do something bad, we're less susceptible to feeling we are bad.

Shame, blame, and guilt are part of the human condition of brokenness. Shame used poorly produces oppressive humiliation; used wisely, shame produces humility and compassion for self and others. Blame used poorly obscures the path to responsibility; used wisely, blame allows for acceptance and change. Guilt used poorly crushes; used wisely, guilt empowers and protects.

The Role of Core Beliefs

I find it virtually impossible to engage in a discussion of shame, blame, and guilt without a corresponding look at the role of core beliefs. Core beliefs are what people hold as truth, most often, I've found, developed in childhood. The way childhood affects these core beliefs is explained in a concept called "attachment theory," which involves the bonding—or lack thereof—that takes place between infants and primary caregivers. Core beliefs revolve around how you feel about yourself and others as well as how you interpret the world you live in. As such, core beliefs provide the filter to determine how shame, blame, and guilt are internalized, strengthening either addiction or recovery.

Terry's core belief about himself was one of worthlessness. He'd learned this at an early age from a father who found fault in every action. Perfection was the standard, and when he was unable to produce those results, his father unequivocally communicated his vast displeasure and disappointment. Juxtaposed to this reaction was his father's delight and pride in regard to his sister, Bethany, who seemingly could do no wrong. In Terry's rebellious teens, an incessant drive to please his father turned into an angry rejection of any standards of conduct at all. From this nucleus formed a twenty-plus-year drug addiction.

Bethany's core belief about herself was one of specialness. As the chosen child in the family, she learned at an early age that she was preferred and protected. Watching what happened to her brother made her feel both smug and terrified; smug that she wasn't him and terrified that she could be. In her insecure middle school years, her drive to protect her preferred position led to a decades-long battle with bulimia and eating disorders.

Almost twenty years ago, I ran across a "Problem Belief Questionnaire" by Clyde M. Feldman, PhD.[5] I found his breakdown of beliefs into seven categories very helpful: power and control; dependent love; approval from others; success and achievement; perfectionism; self-esteem; and trust. He presented a sixty-three-question survey and a scoring system to help people determine where their core beliefs might be problem beliefs. With credit to Dr. Feldman (and the individual it appears Dr. Feldman himself credits, Edmund Bourne, PhD), I'd like to discuss each of these seven areas regarding addiction and specifically as they apply to attitudes of shame, blame, and guilt in recovery.

Power and Control

Addiction wreaks havoc on a person's core beliefs about power and control. A person with a high need for personal power and control can experience tremendous shame and guilt when faced with an addiction. Addiction uses the promise of achieving power and control to infiltrate a person's life. Addiction promises to enhance the very things it will ultimately take away. After an addiction has stripped a person of power and control, it leaves a residue of shame and guilt.

I've seen this play out in eating disorders, especially anorexia. In some cases of anorexia, the person feels as if power and control over their life has been unfairly co-opted by another person, usually a parent. This sense of powerlessness in so many areas of life produces a strong desire to assert control in at least one aspect. To eat or not to eat, what to eat, when to eat, and how much to eat become the avenue for reasserting a semblance of personal power and control. At first the control over food, over hunger and satiation, is a heady, powerful feeling. As control shifts from the person to the eating disorder, the person is left, again, feeling powerless. The one thing that was supposed to right the wrong has turned into something worse.

Some people have a core belief that, to be safe, they must exert power and control over themselves and others. An addiction can falsely promise to advance that agenda, only to tear it to shreds in practice. The person is left with a tattered sense of self, ashamed of and feeling guilty for being "weak," a condition they consider unacceptable. They blame themselves for being weak and "letting" the addiction spin out of control. These are people who fall into the trap of believing if they just "try hard enough," they should be able to manage their addiction.

Others may believe they have no power and are unable to control anything. When an addiction comes and overwhelms them, this seems normal. They feel a sense of "rightness" because it agrees with their faulty worldview. The shame they feel at their own "weakness" is familiar and only strengthened by the addiction. They tend to accept complete and total blame for everything surrounding the addiction because they have always considered themselves responsible—bad things happen because they are bad. Proportionate guilt is difficult to differentiate because they've lived under a cloud of disproportionate guilt for as long as they can remember.

Dependent Love

Feeling capable of giving love to and receiving love from yourself and others is a healthy core belief. Dependent love happens when you believe love is something you can get only from others and never from yourself. You become dependent on other people to provide you with value and worth.

People, however, are notoriously slippery. They act in ways we don't like, they say one thing and do another, they impart hurtful things without thinking, and they have conflicting reasons and motivations for the ways they act. Basing your sense of value and worth on the whims and capricious reasonings of others can be like stepping out onto unstable ground while fraught with anxiety.

Addiction, however, promises the stability of predictable results. Drink this, eat this, smoke this, shoot this, take this, do this and feel better—every time. I have seen this sentiment expressed by those with food addictions. They can speak of their addiction almost like a relationship, as if it is a friend or lover, someone who provides proven comfort. Food can produce the scents and sounds, textures and tastes that mimic the physical sensation of a hug, a kiss, or a caress. Is it any wonder so many people resonate with the term "comfort food"?

Addiction seeks to create dependent relationships by solidifying the addictive relationship and alienating any other. Addiction is ready to step into the breach of a shaky relationship with its lies and false promises. It promotes shame, at the same time claiming if others knew about it, they would surely leave. Addiction buries a person in blame for succumbing to the temptation. It heaps disproportionate guilt for the difficulties in finding and maintaining a viable, loving relationship. Addiction jealously beckons you to love it above all others, including yourself.

Approval from Others

Some people operate under an assumption that the only valid source of approval is someone else. They have been taught that approving of themselves is somehow tainted and must be corroborated to be legitimate. As such, they make decisions and act not as they believe they should but as they believe others think they should. This can involve behaving in diametrically opposite ways, depending on who they are with and whose approval they seek.

This pattern of intentional prevarication fits perfectly with addiction. With an addiction, you must be willing to do anything, say anything, and be anything at any time, as dictated by the addiction. When approval has become your puppet master, an addiction is happy to take over manipulating your strings. As the addictive relationship supplants and pushes away other relationships and others' approval, it becomes the sole source of your sense of belonging. The approval you now seek comes from a different set of people, often those who are actively engaged in their own addictions and naturally approve of yours.

As you begin to distance yourself from that addiction and set of relationships, you may be barraged with disapproval. To reel you back in, they may humiliate you for trying to choose a different path. They may blame you for abandonment as you attempt to leave that former way of life. You may be proclaimed guilty of pronouncing harsh judgment on your former activities and associates. For these crimes, you may find yourself cut off from the approval that came with the addiction. Recovery, then, may seem detached from your lifeline of approval. Though you may be sorely tempted to return to the approval of the addiction, this can become a time when you reevaluate your core beliefs about approval and learn to generate and trust the approval you give to yourself.

Success and Achievement

I call this faulty core belief the what-have-you-done-for-me-lately principle. This is a belief that you are only what you currently produce. Success and achievement must be an ongoing effort, and you absolutely must not rest on your laurels or bask in the glow of past accomplishments. Those occurred yesterday, and your only

161

value comes from what you are doing today and what you will do tomorrow. Failures, setbacks, and reversals are unacceptable impediments. The one glaring problem with this worldview, of course, is that life is full of failures, setbacks, and reversals. So is recovery; they're called relapses.

For years, Bill thought his cocaine habit was contributing to his business success. While high, he was decisive, assertive, and confident. Whenever he came down, Bill wallowed in insecurity, guilt, and fear of his carefully constructed house of cards falling down around him. He told me he had to be successful. That's who he was, who he was brought up to be. Anything less was unacceptable.

When Bill's addiction began to jeopardize his business to the point it was unavoidably obvious, he attacked his recovery with the same set of rigid standards. He substituted business success for recovery success. The pressure he placed on himself to achieve complete and immediate sobriety almost ensured its eventual failure. He felt the only way for him to cope with the shame, blame, and guilt of his addiction was to become sober in record time. When that didn't happen, he struggled with attempting to return and "manage" the addiction, to harness enough of its "power" to resurrect his business. Only after trying this defective strategy multiple times did Bill finally admit he needed to redefine what success and achievement looked like in a post-addiction world.

One lie of addiction is that it creates a false sense of empowerment. At best, the addiction promises control, strength, and competence. At worst, it pledges to obliterate any feelings of powerlessness, weakness, or incompetence, which are feelings to be feared and avoided at all cost. Addiction either makes you feel like a success or shields you from feeling like a failure—with the tottering load of shame, blame, and guilt precariously perched, ready to come crashing down on your head.

Perfectionism

Perfectionists walk an incredibly narrow road. There can be no deviation from the prescribed path, no sidetracks, and certainly no missteps. There can be no slowing or stopping for others, who are expected to keep up and keep straight, regardless. Perfectionists understand the road is going to be difficult and take great pride in navigating it successfully. They must be constantly on guard for any obstacle in the path, any breath of wind that might knock them off their course. Vigilance and an ongoing state of alertness are key.

With perfectionism, there is no standing down, no acceptable periods of relaxation. Perfectionism is, therefore, both exhausting and unattainable. Addiction can creep in and promise a form of momentary relief from the unrelenting anxiety of trying to be perfect. Addiction can also promise to numb those times when the reality of the unattainable becomes overwhelmingly hard to bear. Addiction promises you can spend a few hours looking away from the shame, blame, and guilt nipping at your heels unless you are perfect. Addiction promises to shield you temporarily from the fear that you are, sadly and tragically, like everyone else—flawed, imperfect, unworthy.

Self-Esteem

Angela, who started out this chapter, didn't feel she deserved to be happy. After more probing, I discovered she never had. Any success she'd experienced had been a sort of "cheat," she said. If people really knew who she was or how much work she'd put into it or any number of factors, they would know she didn't deserve success and it would be taken away. How could anything she did be worthy when she wasn't worthy herself?

Angela grew up in a household where nothing she did was right. When she brought home good grades, it was assumed the teacher hadn't applied the proper standards or she'd gotten away with something. Good things were suspect, but bad things were expected because of who she was. She knew who she was—the one who would "never amount to anything." She was the one who would "never be like [her] sister." The one who couldn't "do anything right to save [her] life," even though she always tried.

Angela was deeply ashamed of her addiction; part of her was also incredibly angry. She was angry because being trapped in the addiction proved she was weak and everything that had been said about her was true. All her life, Angela kept trying to "make up" for the mistakes she'd made, and the addiction kept putting her further and further behind. She'd never catch up, and with the weight of the addiction added in, catching up seemed to take more energy than she had. She'd been foolish to think she could ever do or be anything other than a failure. "What good is today," she'd asked, "if I can't have tomorrow?"

Angela's addiction subverted the positive roles of shame, blame, and guilt and used them to convince her she wasn't worth a positive tomorrow. She was especially susceptible to this tactic, since shame, blame, and guilt had always been used as weapons against her while she was growing up. Addiction strips away self-esteem. This can be particularly damaging when you started out with little or none in the first place, as Angela did. (For years, I've been speaking out against the tremendous damage done, especially to children, through the tactics of emotional abuse. My book *Healing the Scars of Emotional Abuse* has been a pivotal resource in this effort for more than twenty years.)[6]

Trust

Some people trust only themselves. They look at others with suspicion, considering them unreliable, at best, or unwilling, at worst, to provide any measure of help or support. Addiction is wholeheartedly in line with that sentiment. The addiction doesn't want you to trust anyone, including yourself. It wants to hold that position of trust exclusively.

A person who is unable to trust others has nowhere to go to work through issues of shame, blame, and guilt. They are their only source of reflection and solace. If they could have provided either, they may not have been so susceptible to the lies of the addiction. When the person who is engaged in addiction is the only person to hold the addiction accountable, failure is virtually assured.

As I've explained previously, failure to trust others usually comes from a faulty attachment between a child and an adult caregiver or parent. For a variety of reasons, the child perceives the adult to be untrustworthy and unable or unwilling to provide for the child's needs. The child learns to handle these needs alone, as best they can.

When recovering from an addiction, a person needs to seek outside help, support, and understanding. Successful recovery, we know at The Center, involves not only individual therapy but also the group environment where people can come together to support the sobriety and healing of others. Those who embrace the group environment and risk the input of others benefit. Those who remain closed off, isolated, and resistant to openness and transparency struggle.

Bearing the burden of shame, blame, and guilt alone can cause a person to stumble. When people are able to trust and share experiences, feelings, thoughts, and impressions, they learn how others have handled and relieved themselves successfully of those burdens. They discover they are not alone. More importantly, they discover they don't need to be.

One hallmark of adulthood is learning what your faulty core beliefs are, understanding where they came from, and figuring out how to adopt healthier attitudes based on an adult's mature understanding instead of a child's incomplete knowledge and judgment. Addiction, in no way, wants to allow for healthy maturation of core beliefs. Instead, it seeks to keep a person trapped in child-hood or adolescent understanding, especially where the concepts of shame, blame, and guilt are concerned. A child may conclude, "I don't deserve to be happy." A mature adult pursues happiness and knows, "I have a right to be."

12

Who Am I Now?

An addiction changes a person, as does any traumatic life event. An addiction, unchecked, seeks to define the scope of that change. Healing from addiction means taking back control. In recovery, people must realize they are not who they were before the addiction, nor are they who they were during the addiction. They can only change who they are in recovery.

"I don't know who I am," Carl said. "I'm not eighteen anymore. I've spent almost twelve years putting my time and energy into something that can no longer be a part of my life. I've got this huge hole, and I'm not sure how to fill it."

"Why do you call it a hole?" I asked.

He looked puzzled by the question. "What else would you call it? I feel like there's this huge infection that's been cut out of me." Carl shrugged. "There's a hole."

"I don't see a hole," I responded. "I see an opportunity."

I could tell he thought I was giving him one of those "therapist," power-of-positive-thinking type of answers. "No, I mean it," I insisted. "When you go to plant a tree, what's the first thing you have to do?"

"Buy the tree," he said flatly, showing he was less than thrilled with this line of conversation.

"Okay, I'll give you that," I conceded. "What's the second thing you need to do?"

Carl thought a minute and then the light came on. He gave a small sideways smile and said, "Dig a hole."

I smiled back. "If you're going to put something in, you need to take something out. If you want to call what's happened to you a hole, okay. Instead of focusing on what you've taken out, why not think about what you'd like to put in?"

Filling in the Hole

In recovery, addiction may not be actively working, but it can be actively speaking, griping, complaining, comparing, undermining. Addiction wants to fill in the hole with the old stuff; after all, it knows that stuff fits because the hole is where it came from. It is all too happy to wriggle right back into the hole and fill it up with the same old putrid stuff. Instead, I've found recovery works best when you actively begin to fill up that hole with healthy attitudes, actions, and activities as much and as soon as you can.

Sometimes old stories are the best. There's a great old story, told several thousand years ago by a man named Jesus. As a Christian, I confess to being partial to his stories. In this story from the book of Luke, Jesus talks about someone with an "impure spirit." (When I use this story with others, I tend to let them decide their own definition of that term. I'm more interested in the overall analogy.) Jesus says, "When an impure spirit comes out of a person, it goes through arid places seeking rest and does not find it. Then it says, 'I will return to the house I left.' When it arrives, it finds the house swept clean and put in order. Then it goes and takes seven other spirits more wicked than itself, and they go in and live there. And the final condition of that person is worse than the first."[1]

The application I try to make by relating this story is the need to not only clean out the bad but also fill in with the good. If you just try to remove the bad, it has a way of coming back with a vengeance. Empty spaces tend to fill up. In recovery, you—and not the addiction—need to be in charge of what fills the hole.

To stimulate your own thinking about healthy attitudes, actions, and activities you can use to fill up holes left from addiction, I've highlighted seven for each category. While there's a plethora of addictive possibilities, human nature is consistent, so I'm confident at least some of these will be applicable, regardless of the addictions you've experienced. I've started with attitudes because they undergird our actions and fuel our activities. When we rip out false beliefs, we need to reconstruct our foundational thinking with healthy attitudes.

Seven Healthy Attitudes

According to a recent Gallup poll, almost nine out of ten Americans believe in God or a "universal spirit."[2] Alcoholics Anonymous uses the term "higher power." As a Christian, I have a worldview that includes a compassionate and gracious God who loves me. Because of this worldview, I believe there is a spiritual side to recovery. So as I present these healthy attitudes, actions, and activities, don't be surprised if I link a thought, an idea, or a concept to spirituality.

1. *I have value and worth.* For some people, an addiction begins as running away from a feeling of worthlessness. The actions of addiction can numb that terrible "truth" of worthlessness in a way real life cannot. For others, addiction erodes existing feelings of value and worth. The result can be the loss of personal value and worth, either because they weren't there in the first place or because the addiction ate them alive.

The first healthy attitude that needs to be discovered or re-instated is an understanding that you have value and worth. If you don't believe that, I'm not sure where the motivation for continued recovery is going to come from. Every human being is born with value and worth, which, according to my worldview, is a gift from God. That gift is yours, whether or not you believe it.

Addiction does not want you to believe it. It wants to be the ultimate power in your life. Whatever your worldview includes—be it God or a universal spirit or a higher power—belief in something outside of yourself and more powerful than your addiction is vital to recovery. When addiction seeks to condemn you, that power can speak up for you.

When your belief in your own value and worth has been restored and supported, you are motivated and encouraged outside of yourself to live your life in that reality. You cannot change the way you lived in the past, but you can determine how you live your life going forward and with what set of attitudes. If addiction has stripped you of your sense of value and worth, isn't it time for you to claim them?

Do you find yourself in the 10 percent of those who don't believe in God or just aren't sure? Do you find yourself in the 90 percent who believe in God but aren't sure how that belief can assist in your recovery? In either circumstance, I encourage you to seek spiritual counsel. At The Center, our mental health professionals understand the power of a spiritual perspective in recovery. Since our founding, we have incorporated emotional, relational, physical, and spiritual concepts into our whole-person care. We work with people to explore the role of spirituality in recovery and have trained pastoral counselors who are able to assist people navigating the spiritual challenges of value, worth, and purpose in life.

2. *I can ask for help.* There was probably a point in your active addiction when you would ask anyone and everyone for help.

There is a difference, however, between asking for help to continue the addiction and asking for help to end it. The addictive mind wasn't above asking for help to stay mired in the addiction; it was only when you decided to leave that the addiction told you that you didn't "deserve" help. Addiction wanted you completely on your own, unsupported, because its influence over you would be that much greater.

Some in recovery may resist asking for help because of a false sense of pride. They may concede the addiction was wrong but are desperately trying to "clean up the mess" on their own. This leaves them stuck in humiliation and blocks their path to humility. Both mind-sets keep them isolated from those who could and would help. A healthy attitude says, "I can ask for help because I recognize I need help" and "I accept that I am worth helping."

In recovery, you learn not only that it's acceptable to ask for help but also what true help is and who is appropriate to receive help from. My worldview encourages me to seek out help from a power higher than myself. For this reason, I love the following Bible passage from the book of James: "If any of you lacks wisdom, you should ask God, who gives generously to all without finding fault, and it will be given to you."[3]

3. *I am not alone.* Addiction, as I've tried to state in numerous ways, is a very lonely place to be. Even if you're surrounded by others in active addiction, at times you wake up alone, feeling alienated and isolated from others. Your user friends are oxymorons—because they're users, they don't have the capacity for true friendship. Because they're addicts, they don't have the current capacity to put anyone above their addiction.

Recovery can also feel lonely. Your family members and nonuser friends may have withdrawn from you during your addiction out of self-preservation. They may have trouble dipping their toes back into the water of relationship with you, having been scalded—perhaps multiple times.

In recovery, however, you are not alone; you are joining a community with, literally, millions of members. In years past, finding others in recovery meant locating a local Alcoholics Anonymous, Narcotics Anonymous, Gamblers Anonymous, or Overeaters Anonymous meeting. Today, through the connective power of the internet, finding others in recovery is as quick as a few keystrokes (though I still recommend attending face-to-face meetings whenever possible in addition to whatever online recovery community you connect with). You might be surprised to find neighbors, coworkers, and even family members within the recovery community.

Within a faith community, you have access to others who share your worldview. Your faith supports you with an understanding that God is with you as well. You might argue that God won't help you because you don't deserve his love. When you hear that voice in the back of your mind, it's the voice of addiction—the voice that uses shame, blame, and guilt against you to chain you back into addictive slavery. Don't listen!

I believe God loves us because he chooses to, not because we've made some sort of "nice" list and avoided the "naughty" list. He's not Santa; he's God. He's all-powerful, and his love is all-powerful and strong enough to withstand adversity—including addiction.

4. *I am grateful for my life.* A life of addiction is a life of regret. In recovery, that feeling of regret can seep into your thoughts and poison your attitude. Regret can cause you to view your life as a waste, as irredeemable. If you no longer appreciate your life, you may be tempted to turn your back on recovery and return to active addiction.

Gratitude helps you find the positive in situations, even negative or painful ones. One skill I teach those in recovery from addiction is how to look for the positive. Even in terrible situations, a person may be able to identify people who cared, made themselves available, or offered what help they could. They may be able to see that hitting rock bottom was when they came to understand the truth of the addiction—a positive insight that led them to repudiate the addiction and reach out for help. When you choose to find the positive, you see negatives in a different light.

Recovery is not a straightforward path, and it will involve suffering—physical, mental, emotional, relational, and spiritual. Addiction does not give up easily. In suffering, you may find it difficult to be grateful for your life. I urge you to create a gratitude list, a way for you to remember all the good and positive things in your life—no matter when they occurred. Some people have kept talismans of special moments or pictures of loved ones to spark the flame of gratitude when it flickers and threatens to go out.

Being grateful for your life doesn't mean glossing over the hard parts. Instead, being grateful means mining those hard parts for jewels of gratitude, even if they are small. Add to your collection wherever possible. Keep them handy. Put them up to the light and remember they are precious and hard won.

5. *I am acceptable, not perfect.* Too many of us have a false belief that to be acceptable, we must be perfect. We have learned this through the negative reactions we've received when we've been less than perfect. What we fail to recognize, however, is how often perfect is defined by another flawed, imperfect human being. Two imperfect human beings trying to define perfection is sort of like another story Jesus told, in which he asked, "Can the blind lead the blind? Will they not both fall into a pit?"[4] Trying to attain perfection to be acceptable is a bottomless pit. Addiction is more than happy for us to continue residing in that pit.

A healthy attitude about self-acceptance is to acknowledge we are not perfect. We cannot be. Sooner or later (in a lot of cases sooner), all of us mess up. The answer when we do is not to despair of ever doing right but to learn from what went wrong. As I've said before, this is how relapse is integrated into recovery.

I can hear some people protest that this attitude isn't healthy because it leaves the door open for justifying relapse after relapse after relapse. A person must be on guard and determine when this attitude is being used by addiction as an excuse. Perhaps the word that needs to be focused on isn't *perfect* but *acceptable*. Our relapses become unacceptable when they happen without us learning anything to continue in recovery. No one is perfect, so being imperfect cannot be handed to addiction as a ready-made barrier to block recovery.

6. *I am lovable.* Some coming out of addiction can feel damaged or tainted by the experience. They may feel dirty or live with feelings of intense shame about what happened during the addiction. Because of these feelings, they may consider themselves "unlovable." They may shun other people to avoid the rejection, or they may attempt to "buy" love from others.

The capacity to give and receive love from others starts first with yourself. One of the pivotal attitude shifts in recovery is when you look yourself in the mirror and can say, "I love you." When you love yourself, you are more able to understand how others could love you as well.

So much is tied up with this four-letter word. Love, in my estimation, is a spiritual characteristic lived out in the everyday thoughts and actions of people like me and you. One of the most famous descriptions of love is found in the Bible: "Love is patient, love is kind. It does not envy, it does not boast, it is not proud. It does not dishonor others, it is not self-seeking, it is not easily angered, it keeps no record of wrongs. Love does not delight in evil but rejoices with the truth. It always protects, always trusts, always hopes, always perseveres."[5] This is a lofty standard, I'll grant you. As recovery is a journey, so is learning to love yourself and others. The goal is to keep moving in the right direction.

7. *I can look forward to the future.* Having an addiction twists your perception of the future. With an addiction, the only future is the next hit, the next drink, the next encounter. The future, then, becomes a series of short-term imperatives. Any vision

beyond those moments of panic and relief is obscured; the future is shrouded. The last thing an addiction wants you to say in recovery is, "I can look forward to the future," especially a future without addiction.

In recovery, as the addiction recedes, people get their long-distance vision back. They can look to the future and look forward to the future. When you can look forward to the future, hope has been restored. As I mentioned earlier, over the years, The Center has adopted a theme verse out of the Bible: "'For I know the plans I have for you,' declares the Lord. 'Plans to prosper you and not to harm you, plans to give you hope and a future.'"[6]

In a strange way, restoring a positive future helps you reconnect to your positive past. This isn't to say the past was all positive; with addiction, it wasn't. Yet I've worked with people who in jettisoning their addictive pasts ended up trashing their complete past. Not everything from the past, though, needs to be turned to ash. I'm reminded of people who have suffered through a natural disaster or a fire. On returning to their homes, they sift through the debris to look for things of value that survived. People may want to torch their entire addictive past, but I encourage them to return, when the coast is clear, and retrieve anything of value they can.

Seven Healthy Actions

With healthy attitudes, a person can begin to take healthy actions. These are actions I've found to be practical and beneficial. Some are emotional actions, several are relational actions, and others are physical actions. I am confident that, as you look over my suggestions, you'll think of others specific to you, your situation, and your recovery. This isn't a list to memorize; it's a list to model.

1. *I practice forgiveness.* No revelation here—you will mess up. I've already spoken at length about the reality of relapse in recovery. When you stumble, and you will at some point and in

some way, forgiveness helps you get back on your feet and moving in the right direction. Forgiveness is a reset because it acknowledges that wrong was done. If nothing was wrong, there would be nothing to forgive.

Did you notice the word *practice*? This is because forgiveness takes practice—and not just in recovery. If you've beaten yourself up over your addiction, treating yourself with kindness, gentleness, and forgiveness probably isn't second nature. At first forgiving yourself may seem strange and awkward.

You may also have trouble forgiving others. This is what I call a grading-on-a-curve mentality, which says because you've messed up, you've earned a low life grade. The only way to get that grade up is to lower everyone else's grade, depressing the "curve." In recovery, some may turn to harsh and rigid judgments against others to elevate self.

The Bible contains a great concept that illustrates this curve mentality well. A man who sees an imperfection, a speck of sawdust in his brother's eye, rushes forward to fix his brother. What the man fails to consider is the wooden plank in his own eye! To truly see so he can help his brother, he must first take the plank out of his own eye.[7] Forgiveness thwarts grade curving and promotes speck removal.

2. *I practice honesty.* The definition of *honesty* is being truthful and free of deceit. These characteristics are the antithesis of addiction. Don't be surprised if your honesty is rusty and you must work at being totally honest, because honesty is an all-or-nothing proposition. A half-truth is, by definition, dishonest and deceitful. In recovery, honesty takes practice, practice, practice.

In my profession, I am regularly astonished by how easily some people can lie. Being dishonest and full of deceit comes as effortlessly as breathing. Lying can be habitual and pathological. Addiction is a pathological liar, and the longer a person has been controlled by it, the more opportunities it has had to train the person in the art of lying.

I believe the AA model of sponsorship is vital to counter addiction's deceitful effects. Sponsors, people who are well acquainted with the lies of addiction, can be the most effective at pointing out those lies. Professional counselors are also useful "truth detectors," but I've seen and relied on the 20/20 vision of the recovery community to spot and call out a lie.

Practicing honesty may require you to retrain your brain and create new, truthful muscle memory. Before passing judgment on yourself or others, you may need to stop and ask yourself, "What is true?" The next steps you take must start from an honest orientation for you to continue in the right direction.

3. *I practice openness.* Being honest with yourself is good but not enough; being honest with others is called openness. Open is the opposite of closed. Connected is the opposite of isolated. To be connected, you need to be open. Addiction wants you open and connected to one thing only. Addiction becomes your companion, your intimate partner, pushing out anyone and anything else. In recovery, addiction, with its feelings of shame and remorse, can argue that being open is a bad idea for you, saying, "If people knew the truth, they'd reject you."

I've repeatedly heard people starting recovery express this fear. What I gently try to remind them is that people already know quite a bit of the truth. They may not know all the *why*, but they've seen and experienced the *what*. Openness allows them to put what they've seen and experienced into context. Those who were so concerned about you weren't crazy, though you may have done everything you could to make them feel that way. Regardless of your protestations or excuses or outright lies, they knew something was terribly wrong, and they were right to be concerned. Instead of shielding those people from pain, your openness can relieve pain, not unlike opening and cleaning a festering wound can help heal it.

Being open means being truthful, perhaps most of all, about your own weaknesses and failings. Addiction promises to hide those weaknesses and failings but can't because everyone has them. True openness, then, relies on humility and a recognition that you can and will fail. Openness is encapsulated in step 10 (personal inventory) of AA.[8] Openness is ongoing. There is no "moral balance" in being open and honest about the small things so you can hide the big things—or vice versa. Again, openness takes practice and may seem risky, but in my experience, relationships that react badly to openness already carry risk.

4. *I eat and drink for nutrition.* I didn't use the word *practice* here, but the concept still applies because eating and drinking for health and nutrition is not always second nature.[9] Depending on the addiction, healthy eating and drinking can require even more practice, and by practice, I mean intentionality.

During an addiction, eating and drinking are co-opted to feed the addiction, and this isn't only in the case of eating disorders. Alcoholics consume a large percentage of calories through alcohol. Drugs suppress natural signals of hunger and fullness. Workaholics jam their bodies full of high-calorie, high-stimulant food and beverages to maximize production. Gamers live on high-carb, high-fat, high-sugar options for the same reason. I cannot recall a single addict who paired their addiction with healthy eating and drinking. Even orthorexics, those obsessed with eating only healthy or safe foods, hold distorted eating and drinking habits based on their skewed view of what is healthy and safe.

Addiction is hard on the body. Intentional nutritional support is, therefore, needed to help the body heal. At The Center, we utilize the expertise of naturopathic and nutritional professionals to assist those in recovery to design healthy eating and drinking patterns, including the use of specifically designed supplementation for recovery. In conjunction, mental health professionals help educate those in recovery about the emotional and psychological effects of addiction on eating and drinking attitudes and actions.

Several years ago, I had the opportunity to meet Dan Chapman, founder and CEO of Redd Remedies, a leading provider of holistic, natural health and wellness solutions. I shared the work we do at The Center and the need I saw for a natural support for brain balance and mood. From our conversation, a professional partnership was born. The Center provided input and was a beta test site for the natural supplement In•Joy, just one of many resources to support healthy recovery.[10]

Through our partnership with Redd Remedies, we understand the powerful benefits of targeted, formulated products to promote physical replenishment after addiction. Brain function, mental clarity, mood regulation, stress reduction, and craving suppression are possible through Redd Remedies' comprehensive line of nutritional supplements. I've been extremely impressed with the work this company has done in the recovery field, including everything from formulations to promote recovery from heroin and opiate addiction using traditional Chinese and Indian herbs to fruit extracts to help with alcohol withdrawal. There are formulations that address the mental and general stress prevalent in recovery as well as products designed to support recovery from anxiety and depression, which are often triggers for addiction and relapse. For those recovering from food and eating addictions, at The Center, we recommend Crave Stop, a product consistently being refined and updated with the latest nutritional breakthroughs, as well as inSea2, to assist with healthy glucose metabolism and insulin production. [11]

I encourage you to work with trusted health-care professionals to evaluate your physical and nutritional health, then incorporate healthy nutritional routines as an integral part of your overall recovery. So much work is being done in the nutritional field to support healthy recovery from addictions, more than I could possibly outline here. The Redd Remedies website is a tremendous resource where you can investigate their latest products, which you can certainly do in conjunction with your own health-care providers. Recovery is enhanced when you give your body the support it needs to heal.

5. *I move for health.* Addiction creates stress, which creates toxins, which contribute to physical illness. Exercise, however, has been shown to be beneficial in stress reduction, detoxification, and increased physical well-being. Those in recovery have multiple reasons to incorporate healthy movement or exercise into their daily routines. Recovery works best when healthy habits replace addictive behaviors.

Another benefit I've seen from regular exercise is the routine. When an addiction is absent, there can be time to fill. I've heard some in recovery complain that they "don't have time" to begin an exercise program, to which I shake my head and remind them how much time they previously devoted to their addiction! Surely, I say, you can take some of that freed-up time and get out and walk, swim, ride a bike, dance in your skivvies in the living room, go to the gym, engage in a favorite sport, garden, you fill in the blank.

The Mayo Clinic has endorsed the following seven benefits of exercise: (1) controls weight; (2) combats health conditions and diseases; (3) improves mood; (4) boosts energy; (5) promotes better sleep; (6) reignites your sex life; and (7) can be fun and social.[12] Each of these seven benefits has a place in a strong and healthy recovery.

6. *I sleep for health.* You just read that exercise promotes better sleep. Early in my schooling, while working as a sleep research associate, I learned how vital sleep is as a physically and psychologically dynamic activity. The body repairs itself during sleep. The mind reorders and resorts itself while turned "off." The Mayo Clinic calls sleep "the foundation for healthy habits." Sleep improves mood and temperament; combats serious health conditions; contributes to healthy hormonal release; allows for important REM (rapid eye movement) sleep, which affects memory and mental focus; reduces body aches and pains; improves immune function; and increases work performance.[13]

Sleep is restorative in general and especially so during recovery. Addiction is disruptive to the sleep cycle. Just ask any person in recovery to explain how their sleep changed during their addiction. They will say they slept longer but felt less rested. They will talk about days they were so high they went without sleep, only to crash or black out for extended periods of time. They will mention conditions such as interrupted sleep, going to sleep but being unable to stay asleep, waking up and being unable to return to sleep. The stress and anxiety of their addictions, they will say, robbed them of sleep unless they self-medicated through the addiction. I've heard some say, "A good night's sleep? What's that? I can't remember the last time I had one."

I encourage those in recovery to work with health-care professionals to evaluate their sleep and design plans for improvement. Those plans can involve simple actions, such as having no caffeine after a certain hour, removing all electronic screens from the bedroom, turning down lights and minimizing noise to create a restful atmosphere, and keeping the bedroom from doubling as a workspace. Those plans can also include nutritional support for rest, along with psychological tools for stress reduction. Sleep is an important component to recovery and should not be relegated to the back burner or shunted to the sideline until you "get around to it."

7. I relax for health. Addiction is awash in stress and anxiety; it thrives in red-alert crisis mode. Many people I've worked with in recovery have cited an especially stressful circumstance as their relapse trigger. This isn't surprising, as stress is also given as a reason to start down a path of addiction in the first place. Stress, then, is an open door to relapse.

Healthy actions involve stress reduction and the important skill of learning how to relax. I say learning because, for some, relaxation is a learned skill. There are a variety of relaxation techniques, usually involving sitting comfortably with your feet on the floor, closing your eyes, and taking slow, rhythmic breaths. Each of these techniques has a moment of stillness, in which the person is encouraged to put aside frantic thoughts and reach for a state of calm.

Stillness, I've found in my life, is a precious commodity. Stillness is ceasing to move physically and mentally. When I stop moving, stop creating my own actions, I discover an awareness of the actions of others. In my stillness comes understanding and knowledge. Reflection, meditation, and contemplation are actions that happen within times of stillness. Stillness can also be the restorative pause before action.

Relaxation, of course, involves more than stillness. It's possible to relax and be very active. Yet I think the heart of relaxation comes when we cease to worry, fret, and strive. Our muscles loosen, our thoughts unwind, we enter a place of stillness where we intentionally refrain from physical and emotional movement. I dare to venture that, through this level of relaxation, people reach the very place they were looking for through their addiction.

Seven Healthy Activities

With healthy attitudes and actions, people can begin to selectively choose to engage in healthy activities. These activities become the new pattern, the new flow of their lives in recovery. This new flow fills up voids and creates its own healthy momentum.

1. *I invest in healthy relationships.* Addiction is expensive; it takes time, energy, and money. In recovery, those can be used to invest in healthy relationships. Sometimes existing relationships need to be restored. Other times new relationships need to be formed around recovery and not addiction. Several years ago, I came up with a list of "relationship essentials" designed to help create and maintain healthy relationships:

- Recognize understanding, acceptance, and affirmation as three critical human needs. Each individually is good, but collectively they bind people together.

- Be vulnerable and willing to take relational risks. Relationships are risky anyway, so use risks to strengthen the relationship.

- Be aware of your own negative responses and recognize they may be separate from what the other person intends.

- Attend to conflict without force, rudeness, or avoidance. Take time to see things from the other person's point of view.

- Forgive yourself and others, recognizing your shared brokenness.

- Build mutual respect first through your own actions by acting in a respectful manner toward yourself and others to model what respect looks like to you.

- Know and keep your boundaries, and respect the boundaries of others.

- Listen with your mind and your heart. Be fully present, and after you listen, you'll be better able to respond.

- Create ongoing bonding experiences by honoring traditions and establishing your own.

- Commit to mutual accountability. Be responsible for your words and actions and be willing to hold others accountable for theirs.

- Practice mutual support and encouragement. Be willing to accept support from others while acknowledging others need support from you.

- Be grateful for the positives. Allow relationships room to breathe and grow.

- Practice self-care. Recognize you do the relationship no good if you deplete yourself in the process.

- Cultivate intimacy. Don't force or demand intimacy, which is beautiful yet fragile.
- Celebrate relationships. Too often we take relationships for granted and fail to celebrate them.

2. *I help others.* Addiction causes people to become intensely self-focused. In recovery, I believe it is beneficial to begin to focus outward, toward others. Helping others can certainly entail existing relationships, but I think there is also benefit in intentionally helping strangers. This could be volunteering at a local hospital, a food bank, or in a faith community.

A word of caution: be aware of your place in recovery and avoid volunteering in places or with activities that could trigger a relapse. You might consider volunteering for a single event to determine if the atmosphere and environment will mesh with where you are in recovery. You could also volunteer to work with animals if you're not quite ready to commit yourself to people. If you've experienced legal complications during your addiction, you may need to adjust your volunteering sights. I say this not to discourage you but to alert you of a possible consequence you may need to factor in.

Along with making a formal commitment to volunteer, I encourage you to develop a more informal daily pledge to serve others, whenever and however you can. This is not to make up in any way for what happened during your addiction. Addiction doesn't come with some sort of balance sheet. Instead, this is so you begin to train yourself to focus on the needs of others and realize you have more power than you think to make a positive difference in the lives of others in big and small ways.

3. *I try new things.* You are emerging from addiction as a different person than you were when you began. The "clothes" that fit you before might not anymore. Don't be afraid to discard them and look for others that fit better. As you reconnect with feelings you've been avoiding through the addiction, pay attention to them. You

may be ready for something completely different because you feel completely different. What you did before may not fit who you are now. Don't be afraid to find a new "container" for the new you.

4. *I work.* Work has a variety of synonyms—labor, toil, task, chore—that may seem negative. However, I have found great value in the work I've been devoted to for more than thirty years. Work provides benefits—from financial stability to a sense of purpose and accomplishment. In an addiction, the "work" was to keep up the addiction, with its stress and chaos. Whenever possible in recovery, I encourage people to devote an appropriate portion of time to work. Depending on the circumstances, this may mean a few hours a week or a full-time job.

I counsel people to avoid believing they are incapable of performing meaningful labor and it's the job of others to take care of them. Employment helps to rekindle a sense of self-sufficiency while contributing to a growing cognition of inherent value. This is not to say that people are only what they produce, but there are valid reasons to engage in meaningful work. Find your reason.

5. *I keep to my schedule.* I believe recovery works best when it has a rhythm. Part of this rhythm is established by the practice of regular meetings. Those early in recovery are encouraged to attend meetings daily. When your time is devoted to healthy, life-affirming activities, there isn't any space for addiction to try to horn in and reassert itself.

When people come to The Center for treatment, we provide a Monday through Saturday schedule and help them create their own schedules for Sundays. Upon discharge, some say they will miss that organized schedule. We work with them to create structure when they go home. I encourage you to assign an activity for each hour in your day, not neglecting rest and relaxation. Empty spaces are invitations to addiction.

6. *I get regular medical and dental care.* Addiction doesn't care about your health, but you need to. In recovery, you may have

medical and dental conditions that will need regular attention. Being open and honest with medical and dental providers can allow them to give you the best care possible as well as be an additional source of accountability for you.

Avoidance is a trick of addiction, so you should intentionally counter it wherever it appears. Recovery means taking care of business—all kinds of business. Don't put off important things or refuse to take responsibility, including for your health. A healthy new life needs professional support.

7. *I daily keep pace with my life.* Recovery is a journey; you need to keep pace daily. I've heard a plethora of complaints about the "daily" part of that equation, as if monitoring your progress is some sort of onerous task. You brush your teeth daily, don't you? You take a shower and comb your hair and eat meals every day. You naturally take care of a variety of things every day without resentment. They're just a part of life.

Daily monitoring of or keeping pace with your life can also be a time of reflection and gratitude. A place to stop, be still, and meditate on the blessings of living. Things may have gone drastically wrong in addiction, but in recovery, there is benefit in remembering daily the things that went and are going right. Recognizing these things can help motivate and encourage you to protect and fight for them.

The first chapter of this book started with the question "Am I an addict?" Answering the first question is important, but more important is how you will answer the question of this last chapter: "Who am I now?" When you were an addict, your addiction overshadowed life's questions and answers. In recovery, you are free to ask and answer your own questions. Use your freedom well. Hold on to that freedom for dear life because your life is precious and worth fighting for.

Ending Thoughts

If I could sit down with you face-to-face, here are the two things I'd want you to know: you are a valuable person and there is a plan and purpose for your life. Whether you believe in God or a universal spirit or a higher power or are unsure of your faith or have no faith at all, I would still try to convince you of those same two things because I believe them with all my heart. I believe they can restore what addiction has taken away.

Addiction very well may have taken parts of your life away. You may think addiction has cost you the life you dreamed of. I would tell you that recovery can be the start of a life you've never imagined. Over the years, I've watched people struggle, fall, and get back up as they found their way to healing. They still had moments of mourning over parts of themselves they lost along the way; they also had moments of sheer joy at the new person they'd become. They suffered but learned and chose to keep moving forward.

There is a saying that goes something like, "Anything worth having is worth fighting for." In my experience, and I know this would be echoed wholeheartedly by so many in the recovery community, healing is worth fighting for. And with addiction as an opponent, a fight is what you'll get.

In that fight, I plead with you not to give up, not to let addiction win. If you asked me why, I would circle back to my first two points: you are a valuable person and there is a plan and purpose for your life. If you don't fight to claim that value, that plan and purpose, addiction will continue to undermine you and take over your life for its purpose, with devastating results.

So, I'll leave you with just a few more questions in confidence that you'll find your answers. Where do you go from here? How do you plan to take what you've learned about yourself, addiction, and recovery and put those lessons to good, positive use? My part of your journey is ending, but your next step has just begun.

Acknowledgments

I would like to acknowledge an amazing group of people who partner with me at The Center • A Place of Hope. These dedicated professionals daily walk alongside those struggling with addiction to help them overcome and to heal and grow. The work is hard, but the rewards are transformational. For this book, I want to acknowledge the partnership of Justin Hartfield and our program director Brian Murphy, both chemical dependency professionals, whose compassion and expertise so greatly contribute to our culture of healing and recovery from addiction.

Notes

Chapter 1 Am I an Addict?

1. "Definition of Addiction," American Society of Addiction Medicine, accessed December 4, 2017, http://www.asam.org/quality-practice/definition-of-addiction.

2. "Definition of Addiction."

3. Ron Breazeale, "Catastrophic Thinking," *Psychology Today*, March 25, 2011, https://www.psychologytoday.com/blog/in-the-face-adversity/201103/catastrophic-thinking.

4. Alcoholics Anonymous, *The Twelve Steps of Alcoholics Anonymous* (New York: Alcoholics Anonymous World Services, 1981), http://www.aa.org/assets/en_US/smf-121_en.pdf.

5. "Am I an Addict?" Narcotics Anonymous World Services, accessed December 5, 2017, http://www.na.org/?ID=ips-an-an-IP7.

6. See John 8:32.

Chapter 2 Why This?

1. Seyyed Salman Alavi et al., "Behavioral Addiction versus Substance Addiction: Correspondence of Psychiatric and Psychological Views," *International Journal of Preventive Medicine* 3 (April 2012): 290–94, https://www.ncbi.nlm.nih.gov/pmc/articles/PMC3354400/.

2. 1 Timothy 5:23 KJV.

3. Ephesians 5:18.

4. Wikipedia, s.v. "CAGE Questionnaire," last modified September 26, 2017, 22:17, https://en.wikipedia.org/wiki/CAGE_questionnaire.

5. "CAGE Questionnaire," National Institute on Alcohol Abuse and Alcoholism, accessed December 5, 2017, https://pubs.niaaa.nih.gov/publications/inscage.htm.

6. From a presentation by Nora D. Volkow, MD, to the Senate Caucus on International Narcotic Control titled "America's Addiction to Opioids: Heroin and Prescription Drug Abuse," May 4, 2014, https://www.drugabuse.gov/about -nida/legislative-activities/testimony-to-congress/2016/americas-addiction-to -opioids-heroin-prescription-drug-abuse.

7. "Prescription Drugs and Cold Medicines," National Institute on Drug Abuse, accessed December 5, 2017, https://www.drugabuse.gov/drugs-abuse/prescription -drugs-cold-medicines.

8. "Prescription Drugs and Cold Medicines."

9. Lia Steakley, "Report Shows over 60 Percent of Americans Don't Follow Doctors' Orders in Taking Prescription Meds," Stanford Medicine, April 25, 2012, http:// scopeblog.stanford.edu/2012/04/25/report-shows-over-60-percent-of-americans-d ont-follow-doctors-orders-in-taking-prescription-meds/.

10. Steakley, "Report Shows over 60 Percent of Americans."

11. Wikipedia, s.v. "Tobacco Advertising," last modified November 15, 2017, 22:07, https://en.wikipedia.org/wiki/Tobacco_advertising.

12. "Current Cigarette Smoking among Adults in the United States," Centers for Disease Control and Prevention, December 1, 2016, https://www.cdc.gov /tobacco/data_statistics/fact_sheets/adult_data/cig_smoking/.

13. "Nicotine Addiction and Your Health," US Department of Health and Human Services, accessed December 5, 2017, https://betobaccofree.hhs.gov /health-effects/nicotine-health/.

14. Clay McNight, "List of Foods and Drinks That Contain Caffeine," LiveStrong.com, October 3, 2017, http://www.livestrong.com/article/245410 -list-of-foods-drink-that-contain-caffeine/.

15. Donald Hensrud, MD, "Nutrition and Healthy Eating," Mayo Clinic, accessed December 5, 2017, http://www.mayoclinic.org/healthy-lifestyle/nutrition -and-healthy-eating/expert-answers/coffee-and-health/faq-20058339.

16. Hensrud, "Nutrition."

17. Certified through the International Association of Eating Disorder Professionals.

18. National Association of Anorexia Nervosa and Associated Disorders, "Eating Disorder Statistics," ANAD.org, accessed January 8, 2017, http://www .anad.org/get-information/about-eating-disorders/eating-disorders-statistics/.

19. "Overweight and Obesity Statistics," National Institute of Diabetes and Digestive and Kidney Diseases, August 2017, https://www.niddk.nih.gov/health -information/health-statistics/Pages/overweight-obesity-statistics.aspx.

20. The story of my recovery from burnout is chronicled in my book *How to De-Stress Your Life* (Grand Rapids: Revell, 2008).

21. Patrick Anselme and Mike J. F. Robinson, "What Motivates Gambling Behavior? Insight into Dopamine's Role," *Frontiers in Behavioral Neuroscience* 7 (December 2, 2013): 182; "Understanding Addiction," HelpGuide.org, accessed December 12, 2017, https://www.helpguide.org/harvard/how-addiction-hijacks-the-brain.htm.

22. Berit Brogaard, "What Happens during an Adrenaline Rush?" LiveStrong .com, April 16, 2015, http://www.livestrong.com/article/203790-what-happens -during-an-adrenaline-rush/.

23. *Online Etymology Dictionary*, s.v. "endorphin," accessed December 12, 2017, http://www.etymonline.com/index.php?term=endorphin.

24. James Titcomb, "Which Country Watches the Most TV in the World?" *The Telegraph*, December 10, 2015, http://www.telegraph.co.uk/technology/news /12043330/Which-country-watches-the-most-TV-in-the-world.html.

25. Shannon Greenwood, Andrew Perrin, and Maeve Duggan, "Social Media Update 2016," Pew Research Center, November 11, 2016, http://www.pewinternet .org/2016/11/11/social-media-update-2016/.

26. Mike Elgan, "Social Media Addiction Is a Bigger Problem than You Think," Computerworld, December 14, 2015, http://www.computerworld.com/article/30 14439/internet/social-media-addiction-is-a-bigger-problem-than-you-think.html.

27. Elgan, "Social Media Addiction."

28. Eric P. S. Baumer et al., "Missing Photos, Suffering Withdrawal, or Finding Freedom? How Experiences of Social Media Non-Use Influence the Likelihood of Reversion," *Social Media + Society* (July–December 2015): 1–15, http://journals .sagepub.com/doi/pdf/10.1177/2056305115614851.

29. Baumer et al., "Missing Photos," 3.

30. Sherry Rauh, "Video Game Addiction No Fun," WebMD, accessed December 12, 2017, http://www.webmd.com/mental-health/addiction/features/video -game-addiction-no-fun#1.

31. Rauh, "Video Game Addiction."

32. Rauh, "Video Game Addiction."

33. Jake Bullinger, "Inside Gaming's Addictive World," 425Business, August 24, 2015, http://425business.com/inside-gamings-addictive-world/.

34. Meredith Somers, "More than Half of Christian Men Admit to Watching Pornography," *Washington Times*, August 24, 2017, http://www.washington times.com/news/2014/aug/24/more-than-half-of-christian-men-admit-to -watching-/.

35. José De-Sola Gutiérrez, Fernando Rodríguez de Fonseca, and Gabriel Rubio, "Cell-Phone Addiction: A Review," *Frontiers in Psychiatry* 7 (2016): 175, https:// www.ncbi.nlm.nih.gov/pmc/articles/PMC5076301/.

36. Kelly Wallace, "10 Signs You Might Be Addicted to Your Smartphone," CNN, November 25, 2014, http://www.cnn.com/2014/11/25/living/10-signs -smartphone-addiction-digital-life/.

37. Lee Rainie, "Cell Phone Ownership Hits 91 Percent of Adults," Pew Research Center, accessed January 8, 2018, http://www.pewresearch.org/fact-tank /2013/06/06/cell-phone-ownership-hits-91-of-adults/.

38. Aaron Smith, "US Smartphone Use in 2015," Pew Research Center, April 1, 2015, http://www.pewinternet.org/2015/04/01/us-smartphone-use-in-2015/.

Chapter 3 Why Me?

1. For an excellent book on attachment disorders, please see Dr. Tim Clinton and Dr. Gary Sibcy, *Attachments: Why You Love, Feel, and Act the Way You Do* (Nashville: Thomas Nelson, 2009).

2. Marci R. Mitchell and Marc N. Potenza, "Addictions and Personality Traits: Impulsivity and Related Constructs," *Current Behavioral Neuroscience Reports* 1 (2014):1–12, https://www.ncbi.nlm.nih.gov/pmc/articles/PMC3996683/.

3. "Genetics and Epigenetics of Addiction," National Institute on Drug Abuse, last updated February 2016, https://www.drugabuse.gov/publications/drugfacts /genetics-epigenetics-addiction.

4. S. P. Farris et al., "Transcriptome Organization for Chronic Alcohol Abuse in Human Brain," *Molecular Psychiatry* 20 (2015): 1428–47, http://www.nature .com/mp/journal/v20/n11/abs/mp2014159a.html.

5. Susan Scutti, "Is Alcoholism Genetic? Scientists Discover Link to a Network of Genes in the Brain," Medical Daily, December 2, 2014, http://www.medicaldaily .com/alcoholism-genetic-scientists-discover-link-network-genes-brain-312668.

6. "Scientists Find Gene Linked to Alcoholism," University of North Carolina School of Medicine, October 19, 2010, http://www.med.unc.edu/www/newsarchive /2010/october/scientists-find-gene-linked-to-alcoholism.

7. *Opioid Addiction 2016 Facts & Figures*, American Society of Addiction Medicine, https://www.asam.org/docs/default-source/advocacy/opioid-addiction -disease-facts-figures.pdf.

Chapter 4 Why Can't I Just Learn to Live with This?

1. Cynthia Rowland McClure, *The Monster Within: Facing an Eating Disorder* (Grand Rapids: Revell, 2002).

Chapter 6 Why Can't I See What This Is Doing to Me?

1. "Drugs, Brains, and Behavior: The Science of Addiction," National Institute on Drug Abuse, accessed December 13, 2017, https://www.drugabuse.gov/publica tions/drugs-brains-behavior-science-addiction/addiction-health.

2. "Stress Effects on the Body," American Psychological Association, accessed December 14, 2017, http://www.apa.org/helpcenter/stress-body.aspx.

3. See Hebrews 11:1.

4. See Matthew 17:20.

Chapter 8 Why Is the First Step So Hard?

1. *Merriam Webster's Collegiate Dictionary*, s.v. "800-pound gorilla."

2. "Gorilla Fact Sheet," World Animal Foundation, accessed January 8, 2018, http://www.worldanimalfoundation.net/f/gorilla.pdf.

3. Alcoholics Anonymous, *The Twelve Steps*.

4. Wikipedia, s.v. "Invictus," last modified December 13, 2017, 9:23, https://en .wikipedia.org/wiki/Invictus.

5. Alcoholics Anonymous, *The Twelve Steps*.

6. "America's Top Fears 2016," Chapman University, October 11, 2016, https:// blogs.chapman.edu/wilkinson/2016/10/11/americas-top-fears-2016/.

7. Brian Cuban, *The Addicted Lawyer: Tales of the Bar, Booze, Blow, and Redemption* (New York: Post Hill Press, 2017), 188.

Chapter 9 Why Isn't the First Step Enough?

1. Cuban, *The Addicted Lawyer*, 217.
2. A. Thomas McLellan et al., "Drug Dependence, a Chronic Medical Illness: Implications for Treatment, Insurances, and Outcomes Evaluation," *Journal of the American Medical Association*, May 12, 2009, https://jpo.wrlc.org/bitstream /handle/11204/3721/Drug%20Dependence%20A%20Chronic%20Medical%20 Illness_Implications%20for%20Treatment%20Insurance%20and%20Outcomes %20Evaluation.pdf?sequence=3.
3. "Drugs, Brains, and Behavior."
4. Alcoholics Anonymous, *Young People and AA* (New York: Alcoholics Anonymous World Services, 2017), https://www.aa.org/assets/en_US/p-4_young peopleandaa.pdf.
5. Christian Hendershot et al., "Relapse Prevention for Addiction Behaviors," *Substance Abuse Treatment, Prevention, and Policy*, https://www.ncbi.nlm.nih .gov/pmc/articles/PMC3163190/.
6. Matthew 6:34.
7. Hendershot et al., "Relapse Prevention."

Chapter 10 How Can I Put My Life Back Together?

1. "Lao Tzu," BBC, accessed December 19, 2017, http://www.bbc.co.uk/world service/learningenglish/movingwords/shortlist/laotzu.shtml.

Chapter 11 Do I Deserve to Put My Life Back Together?

1. *Oxford Dictionaries*, s.v. "shame," accessed December 18, 2017, https://en .oxforddictionaries.com/definition/shame.
2. *Merriam-Webster*, s.v. "humiliate," accessed December 18, 2017, https://www .merriam-webster.com/dictionary/humiliation.
3. Wikipedia, s.v. "Serenity Prayer," last modified December 11, 2017, 17:34, https://en.wikipedia.org/wiki/Serenity_Prayer.
4. Alcoholics Anonymous, *The Twelve Steps*.
5. Clyde M. Feldman, PhD, *Problem Beliefs Questionnaire*, accessed December 18, 2017, http://www.counselingtoolsthatwork.com/files/Download/RELA T6FREE.pdf.
6. Gregory Jantz, *Healing the Scars of Emotional Abuse* (Grand Rapids: Baker Books, 2009).

Chapter 12 Who Am I Now?

1. Luke 11:24–26.
2. Frank Newport, "Most Americans Still Believe in God," Gallup News, June 29, 2016, http://news.gallup.com/poll/193271/americans-believe-god.aspx.
3. James 1:5.
4. Luke 6:39.
5. 1 Corinthians 13:4–7.

6. Jeremiah 29:11.

7. See Matthew 7:2–5.

8. Alcoholics Anonymous, *The Twelve Steps*.

9. Julie Beck, "Less Than 3 Percent of Americans Live a 'Healthy Lifestyle,'" *Atlantic*, March 23, 2016, https://www.theatlantic.com/health/archive/2016/03 /less-than-3-percent-of-americans-live-a-healthy-lifestyle/475065/.

10. For more information, visit https://reddremedies.com/product/in-joy/.

11. For more information, visit https://reddremedies.com/product/crave-stop/.

12. "Exercise: 7 Benefits of Regular Physical Activity," Mayo Clinic, accessed December 20, 2017, http://www.mayoclinic.org/healthy-lifestyle/fitness/in-depth /exercise/art-20048389.

13. Stacey M. Peterson and Brooke L. Werneburg, "Sleep: The Foundation for Healthy Habits," Mayo Clinic, accessed December 20, 2017, http://www.mayo clinic.org/healthy-lifestyle/adult-health/in-depth/sleep-the-foundation-for -healthy-habits/art-20270117.

Gregory L. Jantz, PhD, is a popular speaker and award-winning author of more than twenty-five books, including *Healing the Scars of Childhood Abuse*, *Healing the Scars of Emotional Abuse*, and *Every Woman's Guide to Managing Your Anger*. He is the founder of The Center for Counseling & Health Resources, Inc. (www.aplaceofhope.com), also known as The Center • A Place of Hope, in the state of Washington.

Ann McMurray has partnered with Dr. Jantz for twenty-five years, both in writing collaboration and at The Center • A Place of Hope.

It is possible to become
Whole and Happy Again

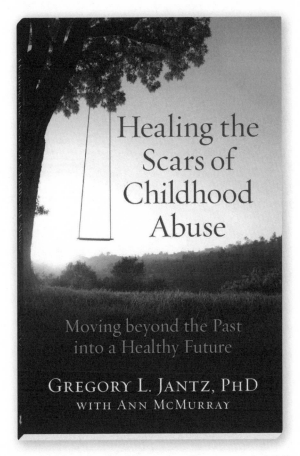

"This book takes on the lasting implications of childhood trauma with empathy and hope. I highly recommend this book to anyone who is ready to heal the past and build a new future."

—MICHAEL GURIAN,
New York Times bestselling author of
The Wonder of Boys and *The Wonder of Girls*

Hope and healing
for the victims
of emotional abuse

 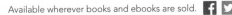